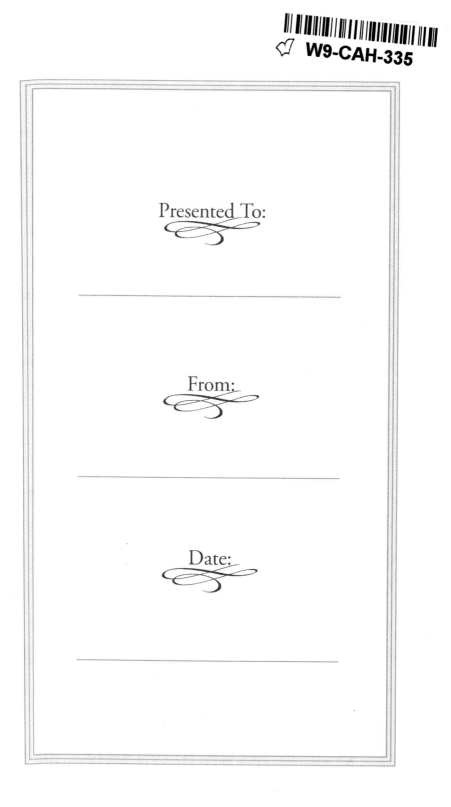

Presented To:

From:

Date:

HOSTING

the

PRESENCE

DESTINY IMAGE BOOKS BY BILL JOHNSON

A Life of Miracles

Dreaming With God

Release the Power of Jesus

Strengthen Yourself in the Lord

The Supernatural Power of a Transformed Mind

When Heaven Invades Earth

Here Comes Heaven

Spiritual Java

Center of the Universe

Momentum

Walking in the Supernatural

AVAILABLE FROM DESTINY IMAGE PUBLISHERS

Bill Johnson

HOSTING

the

PRESENCE

Unveiling Heaven's Agenda

DEDICATION

I dedicate *Hosting the Presence* to Dr. Heidi Baker of Iris Ministries International.

I realize it's not very common to have a book dedicated to the same person who wrote the forward, but I must do so in this case. Heidi Baker is one of the most remarkable individuals I've ever met. Her ability to give herself to the poorest of the poor and the most-broken of the broken makes her stand out in a world of ministries that clamor for success by appealing to the successful. Thankfully, there is a growing number of individuals who serve in the fashion that Heidi has modeled all around the world. They deserve our love and support. But Heidi's uniqueness comes from her ability to also serve the richest of the rich, without the hidden agenda of wanting what they have for her ministry. And this she does with one more extremely rare quality: she doesn't shame them for their success. Instead, she celebrates it.

Before meeting Heidi, I would have said something like this: In a perfect world, there would be one person who embodied the lives of both Mother Theresa and Kathryn Kuhlman. Through the years, I have noticed that Heidi has the same fruit of both of these giants from church history. She lives with equal measures of compassion and power. Apparently, this has become a more perfect world than I had originally thought possible.

I have had the incredible privilege of serving alongside Rolland and Heidi Baker all over the world, including their home base in Mozambique. They continually amaze me. One of the things I've witnessed day after day, year after year, is that they are the same in private as they are in public—humble, passionate, and honoring. Heidi's passion for the Presence of God upon her life is the fuel for everything else she is known for. For this reason, I dedicate this book to her. She models the heart of this book so profoundly.

Iris Ministries now has ministry bases around the world. Rolland and Heidi live in Pemba, Mozambique.

(Of course, she wrote the foreword not knowing what I would do with the dedication.)

ACKNOWLEDGMENTS

I want to thank Mary Berck and Michael Van Tinteren for doing some of the research needed for this book. It was priceless help to me. Kristin Smeltzer and Shara Pradhan, your selfless work in putting together my transcripts was an invaluable help. Judy Franklin, Pam Spinosi, and Dann Farrelly—each of you played a unique role in helping me review and edit this project. Thanks to all.

ENDORSEMENTS

In *Hosting the Presence*, Bill Johnson stirs your heart to go deeper in Him, challenges your mind to embrace the Holy Spirit with a new understanding, and ignites your spirit with a fervent passion to seek and maintain His sweet presence. The testimonies and truth, in these pages of inspiration, will open the eyes of your understanding in a whole new dimension in surrendering to the Holy Spirit. *Hosting the Presence* is a must read for every believer who wants to love and honor Jesus as we were created to.

Dr. Ché Ahn
Senior Pastor, HROCK Church, Pasadena, CA
President, Harvest International Ministry
International Chancellor, Wagner Leadership Institute

One of our highest callings is to host the Presence of the Dove of God. That is my greatest joy and pleasure in this life is to be a perch where this dove can come and have a place of belonging. Over the years I have had the honor of observing the hovering of the Holy Spirit over different churches, gatherings, cities, and nations. But rarely have I seen a person, place, or ministry become a dwelling place where the God of Now builds a nest and not only hovers but lands. This book is filled with lessons and present day history of a tender man of God named Bill Johnson and a risky people called Bethel Church. It is an honor to commend to you the lessons learned by this team of seekers. Join them in being a people who host the Presence of the Heavenly Dove.

James W. Goll
Encounters Network, Prayer Storm, Compassion Acts
Author of *The Seer, A Radical Faith, The Lost Art of Intercession*, and many more

Bill Johnson's new book, *Hosting the Presence*, is a very important book on the most important of topics—experiencing Him. I read the book in one morning and loved it. Thrilled by Bill's personal insights, captured by his insightful one-liners, and challenged as I once again read about other great people of God, and their experiences of Him. This is a book meant for recalibration, calling us back to our first love and warning us not to allow the lesser things rob us of the most important, our relationship with Him. I believe it will become a classic devotional book for our day much as Andrew Murray's writings were for a bygone generation. You won't want to miss this read, buy it and experience Him as you put into practice the wisdom from a modern day general in the faith. I believe if books were allowed to be read in Heaven that this one would be on the best seller list, the mystics from other generations have given it five stars. It would even be reviewed in the New Jerusalem Times.

Randy Clark
Author of *There Is More*
Co-author with Bill Johnson of The Essential Guide to Healing
and *Healing Unplugged*
Founder of Global Awakening and the Apostolic Network of Global Awakening.

Only a handful of men carry the special anointing that Bill Johnson carries to usher in the presence. I have witnessed on many occasions the awesome miracles that result from this grace. So I was totally engrossed and blessed by every page of his new book, *Hosting the Presence*. It ministered to me like no other book I have encountered on the presence of God. The waves of God's glory overwhelmed me as I got captivated by fresh revelations on every page. I never saw Moses or Gideon or David in this manner before. And these revelations kept coming. This will be my manual for the year. I can only say thank you, Bill, and bravo for these revealed treasures. For all believers hungry for more of God's anointing and how to steward it, this is what you've been waiting for. Amazing, awesome, life transforming!

Mahesh Chavda
Sr. Pastor, All Nations Church

CONTENTS

Foreword 17

Introduction 21

1. The Ultimate Assignment 23

2. From a Garden to a Garden 31

3. The Lie of Insignificance 49

4. A Presence that Empowers 65

5. Sneak Previews 81

6. Answers to Ancient Cries 93

7. The Ultimate Prototype 113

8. Red-Letter Revival 131

9. Releasing the Dove 145

10. The Practical Side of His Presence 169

11. Baptism of Fire 183

FOREWORD

Bill Johnson's book, *Hosting the Presence*, is one of the most powerful books that I have ever read. I was undone by Chapter 1 and found myself weeping and crying out for more of the manifest presence of God to rest on my life. I was wrecked with a greater hunger to be fully possessed by the Glory of God and filled with fresh longing for my life to be distinguished by His Presence.

Bill's testimonies of encounters with God reminded me of my own life-changing visitations. I remember one particularly powerful time during a meeting in Toronto, Canada, when I was overshadowed by the Holy Sprit. My friend Randy Clark was preaching, and during his message I felt so desperate for what he was talking about that even without an altar call I ran down to the front and lifted my arms to Jesus. I remember Randy saying that God wanted to know if I wanted the nation of Mozambique. When I screamed back a resounding "Yes!" the Holy Spirit completely undid me and I felt liquid love pulsating through me like electric shocks. It was so powerful that I thought I might die. I couldn't move, walk, or talk for seven days and seven nights. I had to rely on the Body of Christ to help me with everything! During that time I learned about my total dependence not only on Christ, but also on His Body. I felt a heavy, anointed hand rest on my chest above my heart and a river of love repeatedly rolling over me. I had never felt love as powerful as this up to that point in my life.

I later learned from my husband that no one had laid hands on me during this time. It was God Himself putting His burning heart of passionate love within me. This encounter changed my life forever, and I was ruined for anything other than carrying the very heart and presence of Jesus into the darkness of this world. Since that day I have always looked for open doors to release Him. Through Bill's book, the Lord calls us to a place of intimate partnership where we carry His glory daily. I believe that as you read this book God will take you in to a deeper place of yielded affection and openness to the Holy Spirit, and draw you into your own greater supernatural encounters with God. It will teach you to recognize the open doors He has for you, and to release His power and presence through your life.

We have been called to such intimate communion with Him that all things are possible for us who believe, and who have been created to be like Him. As we realize that all the miracles Jesus did on the earth were done as a Man dependent on His heavenly Father, we are invited to believe that our little lives can be used in the same way to carry the awesome glory of God. The death of Jesus on the cross made it possible for humanity to come into a place that had previously been hidden, where humankind could carry the very Presence of God and do all that He did. As I read this book I felt compelled to keep pressing in all the more, until the same things that Jesus did happen in my own life.

As I have listened to Bill's teachings over the years, I have been drawn to press in for new realms of possibility, and to believe that we can see things we never thought we could see through the power of the Holy Spirit. Since meeting Bill in 1997 I have watched the life and power of God flow through him in powerful ways. When I have been at meetings where he has spoken, I have always experienced the manifest presence of God and been drawn into deeper places of abandonment. Watching Bill's personal life of intimacy and abandonment to God has been a great inspiration to me. He is one of the most generous people that Rolland and I have ever met, and he always seeks to empower others to soar in realms of the Holy Spirit. He practices a lifestyle of hunger, intimacy, and constant awareness of God's Presence.

I highly recommend that every believer who longs for possession by Holy Spirit read this book and learn to live a Presence-centered life. Jesus longs to rest upon not just the few, but a whole generation of unstoppable, fearless servant lovers. Those who are willing to wholly yield to His immeasurable, ceaseless love. I believe that as you read this book, Jesus will enlarge your capacity to carry His Presence, ignite your heart with passion, and transition you into new realms of Heaven. You will find yourself in a greater place of yieldedness as you believe that you too can be filled up to all the fullness of God.

May you become the eternal dwelling place of God and soar in your ultimate assignment to be one who hosts the Presence of the King of Glory.

I am undone!

Heidi Baker, PhD
Founding Director, Iris Globe

Introduction

I've never been one to give long introductions to my books—partly because a great number of people don't read introductions. Another reason is that most of what I want to say I'd rather put in the book. But if there's one thing I'd like to draw your attention to in presenting this book to you, it would be Psalm 27:4:

One thing I have asked from the Lord, that I shall seek: that I may dwell in the house of the Lord all the days of my life, to behold the beauty of the Lord and to meditate in His temple.

It's important that we all find the "one thing" that can become the reference point for the rest of the issues of life. And that one thing is the Presence of the Almighty God, resting upon us.

1

The Ultimate
Assignment

There was something different about the atmosphere that surrounded the apostle Peter. He once stood in fear in front of a servant girl, denying that he ever knew Jesus (see Matt. 26:69-70). His lifestyle changed quite dramatically after he was baptized in the Holy Spirit. People not only were healed when he prayed for them, they just seemed to get well when they were near him. The stories of these miracles spread until finally someone noticed his daily routine—he walked to the temple to pray. So they brought the lame and diseased and lined them up along the side of the street so that as he walked by they could be healed by his shadow (see Acts 5:15). It was actually the Presence of God upon him, for *the anointing* is a person. The hope was that his shadow might fall upon them and they would be healed. Shadows have no substance. The shadow was merely the point of contact for their faith. Yet miracles happened with some measure of consistency for the people to develop this pattern.[1]

Jesus was known for healing people with and without prayer. In fact, there were times when it looked as though He was not involved at all in the miracle that happened through Him. From the Gospel records, it seemed to have started when one very sick woman saw the potential of a moment and thought if she could just touch His garment, she would be well. She sensed something was available through a touch that was completely unseen. It had not been done before. Neither was there a record of this process ever being included in Jesus' instructions for "how to get your miracle." He never even implied it was possible. She watched Him work and came to the conclusion that He carried something on His person that could be accessed through touch.

There's no question that faith was at work in her heart. But rarely, if ever, does a person in her condition become aware of their faith. The focus was not on herself. It was on Him. As a result, faith was her normal expression. After touching Him, she found out that her perception was true, and she was healed (see Luke 8:43-48).

The story of that one miracle spread until people everywhere realized that this was a legitimate way of being healed—just touch any part of His clothing. It eventually became the goal of the gathering as the people were *"imploring Him that they might just touch the fringe of His cloak; and* **as many as touched it were being cured"** (Mark 6:56). Imagine crowds of people, sometimes numbering into the thousands, trying to touch this one man's clothing. The Scriptures testify that everyone who touched His clothing *with that in mind* experienced a miracle.

There was a time in the apostle Paul's ministry when he graduated from *miracles* to *extraordinary miracles*. It's amazing that the miracle realm can become so normal that Luke, under the inspiration of the Holy Spirit, had to create a separate category to describe the new miracles. They operate at a higher level of mystery, anointing, and authority. This moment came about in Ephesus. The Scriptures record it this way: *"God was performing extraordinary miracles by the hands of Paul"* (Acts 19:11). It was during this time that the miracles realm exceeded what happened with Jesus where people simply touched His clothing. Now things had developed to such a place that they could take pieces of Paul's clothing to the sick and lame and they would be healed of disease and/or delivered of demons. A unique aspect of the biblical description is that these miracles that happened a great distance from Paul were attributed to being "by the hands of Paul."

These stories are extraordinary. They are glimpses into the ways of the Holy Spirit. We have yet to live in what has already been revealed. I believe it also implies there are ways of the Holy Spirit that are yet to be discovered. These unusual methods reveal how He moves. None of them happened because the people were instructed to behave in such a way, nor was there any suggestion made to hint of the possibility of His presence and power being accessed through these unusual methods. People observed something unseen and responded with faith. Faith sees and responds to unseen realities. Each of the individuals involved in receiving a miracle did so by responding to what they perceived that rested upon these three—Peter, Jesus, and Paul.

This also shows us how the unseen realities of the Kingdom can be accessed through simple faith and obedience. Faith doesn't come from the mind; it comes from the heart. Yet a renewed mind enhances our faith through an understanding of the unseen. It finds its fuel in knowing ways of the Holy Spirit—how He moves. Their unique perspectives on reality, from which they drew their miracle, were not the results of years of study and prayer (which obviously have great value in our lives, but serve another purpose). They were responses to the grace made available in the manifested Presence of God through the Holy Spirit that rested upon people.

It's time for these exceptional stories to no longer be the exception. It's time for them to become the rule—the new norm. And that is the cry of my heart. The apostles learned from Jesus' example that the greatest treasure was the Presence of the Holy Spirit resting upon Him. Learning to host the Presence of God is the biggest challenge of the Christian life.

The Perfect Guest

Consider what Mary and Joseph felt when they heard that Mary would be giving birth to God's Son, Jesus the Christ. He would grow up in their home, be nurtured as their own, and raised for a purpose beyond their comprehension or control. This Jesus was totally God, yet totally man.

If the assignment of raising the Perfect One weren't frightening enough, what would it have felt like to lose Him? It actually happened.

Joseph and Mary had a custom of going to Jerusalem for the feast of the Passover every year. After the festivities were concluded, they made their way back to Nazareth. After traveling a full day they realized that Jesus, who was only 12 years old at the time, wasn't with them. Joseph and Mary had not even completed their job of raising Him when Jesus went missing. He had decided to stay behind in Jerusalem and ask the religious leaders some questions. This He did without asking permission. When they compared records they realized that neither of them had seen Jesus all day. They assumed he was with other relatives or traveling companions in the caravan. This was a moment of great concern. They lost God.

Three days went by before they found Him. I can't imagine that they were really that different from the rest of us. I would first be mad at myself for not being more responsible. Upon finding Him, I would feel relief, but also have somewhere else to place the blame—Jesus Himself. It appears that this is exactly what Joseph and Mary did. Mary asked Jesus, *"Son, why have You done this to us? Look, Your father and I have sought You anxiously"* (Luke 2:48 NKJV). Jesus caused their anxiety. And they put the blame squarely on His shoulders. Now that they were relieved in finding the Son of God, they were also a bit taken back by His lack of concern for their grief. "Why have you done this to us?" Strangely, in the midst of the miracles and extraordinary lifestyle that He exhibited in His adulthood, Jesus would continue causing anxiety.

His response didn't help. In fact, His answer made no sense whatsoever from our perspective. Jesus responded, *"Why did you seek me? Did you not know that I must be about My Father's business?"* (Luke 2:49 NKJV). Isn't it the parents' responsibility to look for their missing child? How were they to have known where He'd be? By implication they were to have known that His ultimate priority in life was doing the Father's business. Jesus was saying that they didn't need to seek Him. He is never missing when He is doing His Father's business. As great an answer as it was, neither Joseph nor Mary understood it.

It is the parents' job to teach their children. To this day the primary responsibility of teaching children does not fall on the shoulders of church or government. It is the God-given assignment to parents. All the other institutions assist. But at this unusual situation, it was the parents' turn to learn. Jesus just revealed earth's priorities from the Father's perspective. This *will* had something to do with the interaction of two worlds—Heaven and earth.

Awakening to Purpose

There is no greater privilege than being a host to God Himself. Neither is there a greater responsibility. Everything about Him is extreme. He is overwhelmingly good, awe-inspiring to the max, and frighteningly wonderful in every possible way. He is powerful yet gentle, both aggressive and subtle, and perfect while embracing us in the midst of our imperfections. Yet few are aware of the assignment to *host Him*. Fewer yet have said yes.

The idea of hosting God may sound strange. He owns everything, including our own bodies. And He certainly doesn't need our permission to go somewhere or do anything. He is God. But He made the earth for humanity and put it under our charge.

If you were renting a home from me, I wouldn't walk into your home without an invitation, or at least without your permission. You would never see me in your kitchen, taking food from your refrigerator and cooking a meal for myself. Why? Even though it is my house, it is under your charge or stewardship. While there may be landlords who would violate such protocol, God is not one of them. He planted us here with a purpose. Yet it's a purpose we can't accomplish without Him. Our true nature and personality will never come to fullness apart from His manifest Presence. Learning to host Him is at the center of our assignment, and it must become our focus so that we can have the success He desires before Jesus returns.

In one moment we find ourselves rejoicing in the dance, arms raised with heads lifted high. In the next we are bowed low, not because someone suggested it would be an appropriate response, but because the fear of God has filled the room. In one moment our mouths are filled with laughter—we have truly discovered *"in [His] presence is fullness of joy"* (Ps. 16:11 NKJV). In the next we find ourselves weeping for no apparent reason. Such is the walk with God. Such is the life of the one who has given himself to host this One.

His longing for partnership is at the core of this issue. It is His heart. He's a Person, not a machine. He longs for fellowship. He loves to love.

My interest in the ever-increasing story of a people suited to carry His presence is in these areas:

- What happens to the person when God rests upon them?

- What is their responsibility in protecting that Presence?

- What is the impact on the world around them?

- How are the ways and nature of God revealed in their encounter?

- What is possible for us through their example?

The Greatest Honor

Hosting God is filled with honor and pleasure, cost and mystery. He is subtle, and even sometimes silent. He can also be extremely obvious, aggressive, and overtly purposeful. He is a guest with an agenda—Father to Son. Heaven to earth. It is still His world—His purposes will be accomplished. This leaves us with a question that has yet to be answered: What generation will host Him until the kingdom of this world becomes the Kingdom of our Lord and Christ? (See Revelation 11:15.)

ENDNOTE

1. The process of how the story of Peter's healing shadow anointing spread is conjecture. The outcome is not, and is ultimately the focus.

2

From a Garden
to a Garden

Our story starts with two people in a garden. The Garden of Eden was as perfect as any place could be. So were its only two human inhabitants, Adam and Eve. They had a unique place in all of creation because they were made in the image of God. That had never happened before. And nothing else had that privileged place in existence. Because of this likeness, the ones made in God's image would rule over the earth and represent Him in personality and function.

Adam and Eve were designed to rule like God. God's way is much different than the common view of ruling today. It is always a rule of protection and empowerment. Even so, Adam and Eve and all their descendants were to represent God on earth to the rest of creation. Their position over the earth was not instead of God, but because of God. He came in the evening to walk and talk with Adam and Eve. Their place of rule was the overflow of their place before God's face as an intimate.

The earth has always belonged to God, but now humankind became His delegated ones to rule in His place. The Gospel of Matthew records a comment from a centurion that gives us a great insight into being *delegated authority*. When Jesus showed interest in healing his servant, the centurion responded:

> *...Just say the word, and my servant will be healed. For I also am a man under authority, with soldiers under me; and I say to this one, "Go!" and he goes, and to another, "Come!" and he comes, and to my slave, "Do this!" and he does it* (Matthew 8:8-9).

This Roman military leader realized that his authority came from being under authority. We can only release the benefit of God's rule flowing through us to the degree that His rule is over us. Jesus was so moved by his response that He acknowledged that this insight gives place to great faith. He also applauded his insight, for its roots are in another kingdom besides Rome—the Kingdom of God. This understanding is paramount to humanity's ability to rule well.

God created everything for His pleasure. He looked over everything He made and enjoyed it. But His interaction with humanity was different than all the rest. It was personal, revealing the richest benefit of being made in His image. A unique moment in this relationship came when God assigned Adam the task of naming all the animals (see Gen. 2:19). Names represent so much more in the Bible than in our culture. A name represents the nature, realm of authority, and the glory assigned to His creation. Whether Adam merely recognized what each animal was given by God or if Adam actually assigned that measure in the name he gave to each animal is not certain. The answer matters very little, as either way Adam was brought into the creation picture as a co-laborer. He was actually given the responsibility to help define the nature of the world he was going to live in. This reveals the heart of God in such a beautiful way. God did not create us to be robots. We were made in His image as co-laborers, working with Him to demonstrate His goodness over all that He made.

The Unhidden Agenda

All that God created was perfect in every way. Not even God could improve its design, function, or purpose. The Garden itself demonstrated Heaven on earth. And the reason for the placement of such an extraordinary place of peace and divine order was extreme—the rebellion of satan brought a scar into what was otherwise a perfect creation. And now peace, the substance of Heaven's atmosphere, was to take on a military function. Disorder had tarnished God's creation. It was now light against darkness, order versus chaos, and glory against that which is inferior, lacking, and hollow.

The first commission in Scripture is given to Adam in the Garden.

> *Be fruitful and multiply, and fill the earth, and subdue it; and rule over the fish of the sea and over the birds of the sky and over every living thing that moves on the earth* (Genesis 1:28).

His immediate responsibility was to tend the Garden. His ultimate responsibility was to bring the same order to the rest of the planet. The implication was that outside of the Garden there was not the same order as existed on the inside. That makes a lot of sense when we remember that the serpent came into the Garden to tempt Adam and Eve. He was already on the planet.

Revelation 12:4 speaks of the dragon being cast to the earth, sweeping one third of the stars with him. It's quite possible that statement describes the fall of satan and his expulsion from Heaven. His arrogance cost him his place as one of the three arch-angels who served God directly, the other two being Michael and Gabriel. We also know that one third of the angels fell with him, which this passage seems to describe. The term "stars" could represent the angels themselves, or it could represent the measure of creation that they had rule over that was now under the influence of the fallen realm. The point is, the realm of darkness already existed on earth before God made Adam, Eve, and the Garden of Eden. He created order in the midst of disorder so that those made in His image might represent Him well by extending the borders of the Garden until the whole planet would be covered by God's rule through His delegated ones.

Never at any time has satan been a threat to God. God is ultimate in power and might, beauty and glory. He is eternal with unlimited measures of all that is good. He is uncreated—has always existed. Satan is limited in every way. God gave him his gifts and abilities at his own creation. There has never been a battle between God and satan. The entire realm of darkness could be forever wiped out with a word. But God chose to defeat him through those made in His own likeness—those who would worship God by choice. Brilliant! It was the issue of worship that brought about his rebellion in the first place.

Satan wanted to be worshiped like God. That rebellion was possible because God gave him a will. The foolish, self-centered choice satan made cost him his position of rule and, more importantly, his place before God in Heaven. His revolt rippled through the angelic realm and ended up bringing one third of the angels with him in his failure.

Spiritual Warfare

I find it fascinating that God didn't give Adam and Eve any instructions on spiritual warfare. There is no known teaching on the power of the name Jesus, no instruction on the power of their praise for God, nor is there any known emphasis on the power of His Word. These tools would be a great benefit later in the story. But right now their entire life was focused on maintaining divine order through relationship with God and spreading it through representing Him well. They were to live responsibly and be productive, have children who would have children who would have children, etc., and expand the borders of the Garden until the planet was covered by their rule. All of this flowed from their fellowship with God, *walking with Him in the cool of the evening.* All of this came from relationship. Satan was never the focus. He didn't need to be, as he had no authority. As yet there was no agreement with the devil.

I become concerned by an *over*emphasis by some on the subject of spiritual warfare. Spiritual conflict is a reality that is not to be ignored. Paul admonishes us to not be unaware of the enemy's devices (see 2 Cor. 2:11). We must be mindful of his tools. But even so, my strength is putting on the full armor of Christ. *Christ is my armor!* Unforgiveness - rejecting Christ's work - is Satanic Weapon!

Adam and Eve, the ones who saw God the clearest, had no instructions on warfare, as their dominion repulsed the enemy in the same way that light drives away darkness without a fight. I can't afford to live in reaction to darkness. If I do, darkness has had a role in setting the agenda for my life. The devil is not worthy of such influence, even in the negative. Jesus lived in response to the Father. I must learn to do the same. That is the only example worth following.

All our actions come from one of two basic emotions—fear or love. Jesus did everything from love. So much of what is called warfare comes out of fear. I've done it more than I care to admit. We would never worship or give honor to the devil. But remember, like the child needing attention in the classroom, if he can't get it for something good, then at least he'll get it for something bad.

The devil doesn't mind negative attention. He'll let us chase him all day long in the name of "warfare." But it's a place of weakness. God calls us into a place of strength—rediscovering our place in the Garden, walking with Him *in the cool of the evening*. It is from that place of intimacy that true warfare is experienced. Perhaps it was for that reason that David, Israel's great warrior and king, wrote, *"You prepare a table before me in the presence of my enemies"* (Ps. 23:5). The place of fellowship and intimacy with God is seen as the table of the Lord—yet it is placed in front of his enemies.

This is a strange picture indeed. But until we understand this concept, we will unintentionally elevate the devil's place much higher than it should be. This kind of romance strikes terror in the heart of the devil and his hosts. At this table of fellowship, our relationship with God deepens and overflows into a life of victory in conflict with the powers of darkness.

The creation of humankind is in a sense the beginning of such a romance. We were created in His image, *for intimacy*, that our dominion over the earth might be expressed through loving relationship with God. It is from this revelation of dominion through love that we are to learn to walk as His ambassadors, thus defeating the "Prince of this world." The stage was set for all of the powers of darkness to fall as Adam and Eve exercised their godly influence over creation. But instead, *they* fell.

The Perfect Landlord

Satan couldn't come into the Garden of Eden and violently take possession of Adam and Eve. That would have been a laughable impossibility. He had no authority or dominion where he had no agreement, either in the Garden or in Adam and Eve. Dominion is power. And since humanity was given the keys of dominion over the planet, the devil would have to get authority from humans.

At this point in the story their experience was much like what Israel was to experience later in the unfolding story of redemption. God had given the entire Promised Land to the children of Israel. It all belonged to them all at once. It was their inheritance by promise. But they possessed only what they had the ability to manage. The expression of God's dominion flowed through them according to their ability to rule well. They ruled well, according to how well they were ruled. God told them why He wouldn't give it to them all at once—the beasts would become too numerous for them (see Exod. 23:29; Deut. 7:22). They were to grow into possessing the fullness of their inheritance.

The same principle applies to us today. From the Garden of Eden to Israel and the Promised Land to the believers of this hour, it's all ours. But what we possess now is according to our capacity to steward in the way that He would. Many have concluded that our lack is the will of God, as though God designed the Gospel to be lived differently during modern times versus biblical times. Nonsense. It is still biblical times.

Now in the same way God had given Adam and Eve the entire planet to rule over, they only had possession of the Garden of Eden. There is always a difference between what's in our account and what's in our possession. The rest would be brought under their charge as they multiplied and increased their ability to represent God well. This would be seen in manifesting dominion over the entire planet. They, too, were to grow into their inheritance. They owned it all by promise. But their control was equal to their maturity. They possessed only what they could steward well.

Because the devil had no authority over Adam and Eve, all he could do was talk. He suggested that they eat the forbidden fruit, as it would make them like God. And they listened. Adam and Eve tried to become like God, but they did so through disobedience. And that disobedience cost them what they already had by design—Godlikeness. When we try to get through our efforts what we already have by grace, we voluntarily put ourselves under the power of law. This was the devil's attempt to get Adam and Eve to agree with him in opposition to God, thus empowering the devil, himself. Through agreement, he is enabled to *kill, steal, and destroy* (see John 10:10). It's important to realize that even today satan is empowered through our agreement.

Adam and Eve's assignment to rule was interrupted when they ate the forbidden fruit. Paul later said, *"You are slaves of the one whom you obey"* (Rom. 6:16). Through their act of rebellion they became the possession of the father of rebellion. The slave owner then became the one who possessed all that Adam owned. That includes the dominion over the planet. Adam's position of rule became part of the devil's spoil. God's plan of redemption would be needed: *"I will put enmity between you and the woman, and between your seed and her Seed; He shall bruise your head, and you shall bruise His heel"* (Gen. 3:15 NKJV). Jesus came to reclaim all that was lost.

Satan's Attempt to Spoil

Jesus came to earth for a number of reasons. But at the top of the list He was to take upon Himself humanity's penalty for sin and take back what Adam had given away so carelessly. Luke 19:10 says that Jesus came *"to seek and to save that which was lost."* People were lost because of sin; so was their place of rule over God's creation. Jesus came to recapture both.

Satan has always tried to destroy a deliverer after they've been born. He no doubt picks up on the prophetic decrees and puts together his plans to destroy God's intention to deliver His people. It was the devil who inspired the killing of the babies in Egypt when Moses was born. He failed, and Moses rose up to be the great deliverer. He inspired Herod to the kill babies in Bethlehem in an attempt to kill Jesus, the ultimate deliverer. He failed again (see Matt. 2:16-18). And then the devil tried to derail the plan of redemption by getting the Son of God to use His authority for self-preservation. This happened at the end of Jesus' 40-day fast. The devil showed up to tempt Jesus to compromise by turning a stone into bread to satisfy His hunger.

Interestingly, satan knew Jesus had the ability to perform that miracle. When Jesus turned down that idea, the devil just tried to get Him to out and out fail by worshiping him. He knew he wasn't worthy of Jesus' worship, nor would such an act be appealing to Jesus, but he also knew that Jesus had come to reclaim the authority that humanity had given away. Satan offered it back to Him saying:

All this authority I will give You, and their glory; for this has been delivered to me, and I give it to whomever I wish. Therefore, if You will worship before me, all will be Yours (Luke 4:6-8 NKJV).

Notice the phrase *"for this has been delivered to me."* Satan could not steal it. It was forfeited over to satan when Adam left God's dominion for the sentence of death. This happened in much the same way as when Esau gave away his inheritance (long term) for the gratification of a meal (immediate) (see Gen. 25:29-34). It was an abandonment of a call, purpose, and inheritance.

The dialogue between Jesus and satan was fascinating. It was as though the devil was saying to Jesus, "I know what You came for. You know what I want. Worship me, and I'll give back the keys of authority that You came for." The devil blinked, so to speak. In this moment, he acknowledged that he knew what Jesus came for. Keys! Jesus held His course, rejecting the opportunity for any kind of shortcut to victory. He had come to die, and in doing so, He would reclaim the keys of authority that God gave to Adam in the Garden.

The whole issue of placing man in the Garden was to create the context in which satan would be defeated by man. God in His sovereignty allowed the devil to set up his rule on planet earth because His intention was to bring eternal judgment to the devil through humankind. In particular, this would happen through the fruitfulness that comes from the intimate co-laboring of God and man.

After Adam and Eve sinned, defeating the devil became an impossibility, humanly speaking. For this reason, it was necessary for Jesus not only to die in our place, but also to live life as a man, with our same restrictions, limitations, temptations, feelings, etc., so that His victorious life was also as a human. There's no contest in a conflict between God and satan. It has always been about the devil and man—those made in the image of God. Jesus had to live as a man, yet not yield to sin. His death was valuable only if He was sinless, for the sinner deserves to die. He had to be the spotless Lamb.

The Ultimate Conflict

Jesus is the eternal Son of God. He is not a created being who somehow ascended to divinity, as some cults claim. He is entirely God, entirely man. But both His life and death were lived as man. What that means is that He set aside His divinity to live as a man. He was without sin and was completely dependent on the Holy Spirit. In doing this, He became a model that we could follow. If He did His great miracles as God, I'm still impressed. But I'm impressed as an observer. When I discover that He did them as man, then suddenly I am completely unsatisfied with life as I've known it. I am now compelled to follow this Jesus until the same things start happening in my life.

Remember, there is no contest in a battle between God and satan. The devil is nothing compared with the Almighty One. The battle was to be between the devil and man, the ones made in God's image. When sin entered the human condition, it became necessary for God's Son to become a man to fight on our behalf. It was an unusual fight. First, He displayed absolute authority over the powers of darkness by healing and delivering every person who came to Him. Secondly, He lived victoriously and purely. There was nothing of sin that was enticing to Jesus because there was nothing in Jesus that had value for sin. Thirdly, He used His authority only for serving others. He did not use His power for Himself. And finally, He did the unthinkable: He gave Himself up to die in our place. That sounds like a strange way to win a war, but it was key. In doing so, He gave Himself entirely to bring salvation to all humanity. For He couldn't even raise Himself from the dead—He had become sin! (See Second Corinthians 5:21.) He was dependent upon God to raise Him from the dead in the same measure we are dependent upon God to save us once we believe. We cannot save ourselves. Even the faith that brings salvation is a gift from God.

The ultimate conflict was between satan and Jesus the man. By giving Himself to die in our place, He satisfied all requirements of the Law for the death of the sinner— *"the soul that sins shall die"* (Ezek. 18:20). He not only died for us, He died *as* us.

Satan's Ignorance

One of the beautiful truths, so often overlooked, is that on his best day the devil can only play into God's hand. Knowing the devil's hatred for humanity, and knowing His hatred for the Son of God, it was easy to set the devil up to crucify Jesus. It's important to note that the devil didn't take Jesus' life. Jesus laid it down (see 1 John 3:16). On numerous occasions the religious leaders planned to kill Jesus. But He had the habit of disappearing while they were pursuing Him. It wasn't the right time for Him to die. When the time was right, He gave Himself as a sheep to be slaughtered. Had the devil known that killing Jesus the Christ (the Anointed One) would make it possible for millions of "anointed ones" to fill the earth as the fruit of Jesus' death, he never would have crucified Him.

> *Yet we do speak wisdom among those who are mature; a wisdom, however, not of this age nor of **the rulers of this age,** who are passing away; but we speak **God's wisdom in a mystery,** the hidden wisdom which God **predestined before the ages to our glory;** the wisdom which none of the rulers of this age has understood; for **if they had understood it they would not have crucified the Lord of glory** (1 Corinthians 2:6-8).*

There are four things we should take note of from these verses. I've highlighted them in bold. First look at the fact that the rulers of the age are passing away, which means they are being "abolished." Second, God's wisdom is a mystery, hidden until He chooses to unveil it. Third, the purpose of the mystery being unveiled is for the glory of humankind! And finally, the key to realizing the potential of this mystery is the crucifixion of Christ! The death on the Cross made it possible for humanity to come into a place with God that had been hidden for ages, a place where humankind, which is not independent of God, but completely dependent upon Him, comes into glory. This amazing accomplishment is because of the Cross. The death of Christ is something satan never would have pursued had he realized the outcome.

The Ultimate Victory

Think about it: Jesus not only died *for* us, He died *as* us. He became sin, our sin, so that we might become the righteousness of Christ (see 2 Cor. 5:21). With that being the case, His victory is our victory. As we receive the work of Christ on the Cross for salvation by faith, we become grafted into Jesus' personal victory over sin, the devil, death, and the grave. Jesus defeated the devil with His sinless life, defeated him in His death by paying for our sins with His blood, and again, in the resurrection, by rising triumphant with the keys of authority over death and hell, as well as everything else that God originally intended for man that will be revealed in the ages to come. Jesus, the victorious One, declared, *"All authority has been given to Me in heaven and on earth. Go therefore..."* (Matt. 28:18-19). In other words: *I got the keys back! Now go use them and reclaim humankind.*

It is in this moment that Jesus fulfills the promise He gave to His disciples when He said, *"I will give you the keys of the kingdom of heaven"* (Matt. 16:19). God never cancelled the original plan. It could only be fully realized once and for all after the resurrection and ascension of Jesus. Another thing to take note of: If Jesus has all authority, then the devil has none! We have then been completely restored to the original assignment of ruling as a people made in His image, people who would learn how to enforce the victory obtained at Calvary: *"The God of peace will soon crush satan under your feet"* (Rom. 16:20).

His people are to manifest the beauty of His rule to a world in unbelief. We have been chosen for this purpose. Not because we're better, but because we're the ones who signed up for the ultimate quest. He enlists everyone who is *available* to learn to carry His presence until all is changed.

The Designer Has Heart

Everything God created was made for His pleasure. He is a God of extravagant joy. He enjoys everything He made. Humanity has a unique place in His creation, though, in that we are the only part of His creation actually made like God. Likeness was made for the purpose of fellowship—intimate communion. Through relationship with God, the finite ones would be grafted into His eternal perfect past and obtain through promise an eternal perfect future. Even the realm of impossibilities could be breached by those created to be like Him. *"All things are possible to him who believes"* (Mark 9:23). No other part of creation has been given access to that realm. We have been invited in a "place" known only by God.

The heart of God must be celebrated at this point: He longs for partnership. He risked everything to have that one treasure—those who would worship Him, not as robots, not merely out of command, but out of relationship.

The Ultimate Plan

We were designed to rule like God rules—in generosity and kindness, not self-serving, but always for the higher good of others. We are to rule over creation, over darkness—that we might plunder the powers of darkness and establish the rule of Jesus wherever we go by preaching the Gospel of the Kingdom. *Kingdom* means "King's domain." In the original purpose of God, humankind was to rule over creation. But then sin entered our domain, refining our task to that which affects eternity. Because of sin, creation has been infected by darkness—disease, sickness, afflicting spirits, poverty, natural disasters, demonic influence, etc. While our rule is still over creation, it has become focused on exposing and undoing the works of the devil. That is the ministry of Jesus that we inherited in His commission. That is the intended fruit of the Christian life. If I have a power encounter with God, which we are required to pursue, then I am equipped to give it away to others. This is the ministry of Jesus—use the power and authority of God to carry on the ministry of Jesus, in the way that Jesus did it. The invasion of God into impossible situations comes through a people who have received power from on high and have learned to release it into the circumstances of life.

The heart of God is for partnership with His created likeness. He's the ultimate King who loves to empower. His heart from day one was to have a people who lived like Him, loved like Him, created and ruled like Him. From day one, God's desire has been to be with His creation as the invited Landlord to look over their increased capacity to rule, making this world like His. In His world, His glory is the center. The more people carry His Presence into all the earth as joyful servants of the Most High, the more we will be positioned to see one of Heaven's major mile markers—the earth covered with the glory of the Lord.

The Ultimate Challenge

Our story started in a garden. God walked with Adam in the cool of the night. Fellowship. Communion. Companionship. Partnership. But it ended because of sin. But then it started again. This time was also in a garden.

*Now in **the place where He was crucified there was a garden**, and in the garden a new tomb in which no one had yet been laid. ...Now on the first day of the week Mary Magdalene came early to the tomb, while it was still dark, and saw the stone already taken away from the tomb. ...But Mary was standing outside the tomb weeping; and so, as she wept, she stooped and looked into the tomb; and she saw two angels in white sitting, one at the head and one at the feet, where the body of Jesus had been lying. And they said to her, "Woman, why are you weeping?" She said to them, "Because they have taken away my Lord, and I do not know where they have laid Him." When she had said this, she turned around and saw Jesus standing there, and did not know that it was Jesus.*

Jesus said to her, "Woman, why are you weeping? Whom are you seeking?" Supposing Him to be the gardener, she said to Him, "Sir, if you have carried Him away, tell me where you have laid Him, and I will take Him away." Jesus said to her, "Mary!" She turned and said to Him in Hebrew, "Rabboni!" (which means, Teacher). Jesus said to her, "Stop clinging to Me, for I have not yet ascended to the Father; but go to My brethren and say to them, 'I ascend to My Father and your Father, and My God and your God'" (John 19:41; 20:1,11-17).

In a very real sense Jesus was actually born twice. The first time was His natural birth through the Virgin Mary. The second was His resurrection.

*But **God raised Him from the dead.**... And we preach to you the good news of the promise made to the fathers, that God has fulfilled this promise to our children in that He raised up Jesus, as it is also written in the second Psalm, "You are my son; **today I have begotten you**"* (Acts 13:30, 32-33).

In this passage we see that His resurrection was actually considered a birth—the first born from the dead (see Col. 1:18; Rev. 1:5). He was not the first to be raised from the dead. He raised many, Himself. He was the first to be raised from the dead *to die no more.* Our conversion follows in the same line: His resurrection DNA is our DNA. He is the *first fruits* of those who sleep (see 1 Cor. 15:20). First fruits come in the beginning of the harvest. This term indicates that His resurrection from the dead was a prophecy that a great harvest is following in the same likeness as His resurrection! We are that harvest. And that harvest continues and increases until His return.

One of the fascinating parts of this story illustrates what I believe to be the central theme of Scripture, and thus the purpose for this book. It's about the Presence.

The first person to touch Jesus in His natural birth was obviously Mary, the virgin. But who was the first to touch Him at His second birth—His resurrection from the dead? Mary Magdalene! She's the one who had seven demons cast out of her and was healed of infirmities (see Mark 16:9)! The Virgin Mary, representing purity and all that is right, welcomed Jesus into the world for His role of fulfilling the Law and becoming the perfect sacrifice. Mary Magdalene, the one who had been sick and tormented by devils, represents the unanswerable needs of the spirit, soul, and body. She welcomed Him into the world for His role of building a family out of the least pure or qualified in any way. The Virgin introduced the One who would close out the dispensation of the Law. The tormented one introduced Jesus into the season of grace where everyone would be welcomed.

In the first Garden, the presence was taken for granted. God walked in the Garden one more time after Adam and Eve ate of the forbidden fruit. Their eyes were opened to their condition and they covered themselves with fig leaves to hide their nakedness. Then they hid from God, Himself (see Gen. 3:8). It was the last time we hear of God walking in the Garden to be with man.

In this garden, Mary would make sure that that mistake would not be repeated. She grabbed the resurrected Christ and wouldn't let go, until Jesus informed her that He had not even ascended to the Father yet (see John 20:17). Jesus' promise of sending the Holy Spirit would now have to take on very practical expression for this one who had to have more of God. She had found the one thing—the Presence of God.

3

THE LIE OF INSIGNIFICANCE

After God gave Moses a most impossible assignment, Moses asked God the question, *"Who am I?"* (Exod. 3:11). The same question has been asked countless times since. Any time we look to ourselves, we will buy into the lie of insignificance. Moses knew he lacked all the necessary qualifications that one should have to be used by God for something so significant as leading God's own people out of slavery into freedom. When God chooses any of us for something like this, the same question should come to mind. It will if we see the call of God correctly. But God, knowing Moses intimately, was neither troubled nor impressed with who Moses was or wasn't. It was a non-essential. *"Certainly I will be with you"* was God's reply (Exod. 3:12).

Initially it looks like God ignored Moses' "Who am I?" question. But perhaps He didn't. It seems that he was letting Moses know that his whole identity was not to be in his skills, training, or popularity. It wasn't his gifts or even his anointing. It boiled down to one thing: "You're the one I want to be with." Who was Moses? The guy God liked to hang around. Moses may not have known who he was. But God knew *whose he was.*

Both qualifications and significance appear different here on earth than from Heaven's perspective. Just as humility welcomes exaltation, so weakness qualifies us for strength. And striving for significance will actually undermine our significance. When Jesus wanted to be baptized in water by John, John knew he wasn't qualified (see Matt. 3:14). But when you're willing to do what you're unqualified to do, that's what qualifies you. And it was the same for Moses. But the deciding factor on Moses' qualifications went beyond even his willingness to obey. It came down to one thing—who would go with Him.

A Journey Beyond Reason

Many if not most Jews hold Moses in the highest place of respect as compared with any other individual in their history. And for good reason. He brought the Law to them (the Word from God), he led them through the wilderness to their inheritance, and equal in importance from my perspective, he modeled a yielded life. His encounters with God remain a high-water mark.

Moses was God's answer to Israel's cry for deliverance. God often answers the prayers of His people by raising up a person He favors.

So **God heard their groaning; and God remembered His covenant** with Abraham, Isaac, and Jacob. God saw the sons of Israel, and God **took notice** of them (Exodus 2:24-25).

The very next verse says, *"Now Moses...."* God did the same thing many years later in making David king of Israel.

*And David realized that the Lord had **established him as king** over Israel, and that He had exalted his kingdom for the sake of His people Israel* (2 Samuel 5:12).

David experienced the favor of God in extraordinary ways, all because of His intended "trickle-down effect," although in God's Kingdom, things do not diminish as they trickle down. When Solomon became king, he spoke of God's blessing on Israel because they were filled with joy and gladness as a result of God's choice of David as their leader.

*Then they went to their tents **joyful and glad** of heart for all the **goodness** that the Lord had shown to **David His servant and to Israel** His people* (1 Kings 8:66).

The point is this: God often chooses people knowing that they are the key to touching other people's lives. Everyone reading this book was chosen first because of God's love for you. But make no mistake. You are uniquely positioned in this world because of the cry of other people. His favor is upon you so you can be a part of His plan of distributing that same favor to others.

When it says He *took notice of them*, He used the Hebrew word *yada*. This is sometimes used to describe intimate relationships. It is the word that means *to know*. But it means more than a grasping of concepts mentally. It emphasizes *experience* as an essential part of *knowing*. God took notice of Israel by setting them up to become a nation that God would know, who in the same way would experientially know their God. He put them in a place of extreme favor by raising up a man of extreme favor. What He was about to do *to* Moses, He was planning to do *through* Moses—bring a nation into significance through real worship. A deep place of intimacy with God was going to open in a way that

51

had never been experienced by a man, let alone a nation. It would be up to Israel to take advantage of such an invitation.

The Man Beyond Reason

Moses lived for 120 years—40 years in Pharaoh's house raised as a son, 40 years in the wilderness leading sheep, and 40 years leading Israel to the Promised Land. If the first 80 years weren't extreme enough, from the palace to the wilderness, the last 40 years were even more so—success and failure, visitations and encounters with God followed by horrible run-ins with the demonic realm, the worship of false gods and the corresponding devilish activity. His conversation with Pharaoh alone is enough on which to write a book. God actually told Moses, *"I have made you as God to Pharaoh"* (Exod. 7:1 NKJV). That's quite a statement for God to say to someone. Unlike anyone previous, God positioned Himself to do as Moses acted and/or declared. It's a rare thing to find God so willing to make Himself vulnerable to a man. But it is His heart to have that kind of relationship with man. All meaningful relationships require such vulnerability.

Moses was about to become a prototype. Of no one else did God ever say, *"Since that time no prophet has risen in Israel like Moses, **whom the Lord knew face to face**"* (Deut. 34:10, emphasis mine). Moses is now taking his place in history alongside Abraham, who God called His friend. But the description He has for His relationship with Moses has a bit more intimacy implied— *face to face.*

God draws us into our destinies by revealing Himself to us. It is the Spirit of revelation where it matters most. Such a revelation creates greater hunger in us—hunger that can only be satisfied by Him. Revelation comes piece by piece, layer upon layer, to generation after generation. Moses stepped into a dimension of God that was new to humankind.

*God spoke further to Moses and said to him, "I am the Lord; and I appeared to Abraham, Isaac, and Jacob, as God Almighty, but **by My name, Lord, I did not make Myself known** to them"* (Exodus 6:2-3,).

God revealed Himself to Moses in a way that not even Abraham, the father of faith, had received. And God was letting Moses know the place of favor he had entered into. Each bit of increased understanding is both an invitation for relationship and a new high-water mark to be sustained by the following generation.

*The secret things belong to the Lord our God, but **the things revealed belong to us and to our sons forever**, that we may observe all the words of this law* (Deuteronomy 29:29).

In other words, Moses inherited the revelation of God's nature that He gave to Abraham. He knew already that God was the Almighty One. But now Moses would receive an additional insight that would shape Israel's entire future. God revealed Himself as *Lord*, which is translated *Yhvh*, or *Jehovah*, the proper name of the God of Israel. This would be the name by which God would be known from this point on by His chosen people.

Revelation is initially for relationship and ultimately for the transformation of our lives. We are transformed by a renewed mind (see Rom. 12:2). And transformed people transform cities.

God is not that interested in our increased understanding of concepts if there's no relationship increasing with it. When God gives us revelation, He is inviting us to a new place of experience—knowing Him. *"To know the love of Christ which surpasses knowledge, that you may be filled up to all the fullness of God"* (Eph. 3:19). This verse states that we can know, by *experience*, what surpasses knowledge or more specifically, *comprehension*.

Moses' role was a frightening one for sure. But he was unique—unique in the sense that he responded to God as few have in history. My football coach would have described him as one who gave 110 percent—more than what is seemingly possible. The verse *"many are called, but few are chosen"* (Matt. 22:14) comes to mind in this context. His response to God moved Him out of the *what's possible* position to a *highly favored* position. So much of the increased favor we get from God is really according to what we've done with the favor we already have. Moses had been called, but now he was chosen. He was one who took what God offered and ran with it with what some might consider *reckless abandon*.

Remember now, Moses was the one God liked to be with. What kind of assignment did God give to him? We know he was to bring Israel out of Egypt, out of the place of slavery to freedom. But what really was the heart of the assignment? *"Let My people go, that they may serve Me."* This is repeated numerous times (see Exod. 7:16; 8:1,20; 9:1,13; 10:3). This word *serve* is also used for the word "worship." Israel has a wonderful picture of the combination of work and worship in their experience that is rare in the church's understanding today. The specific focus of this call was for Moses to bring Israel out of Egypt's captivity into another place in order that they might worship God with sacrifices. It is appropriate that the one who would one day become a *face-to-face* man would be the one with this assignment.

Presence and Worship

King David would later discover some things about God's response to worship that were unknown in Moses' time. Each generation has access to more than the previous. It is God's law of compound interest. Specifically, David recognized how God responds to the praises of His people. God responds with His

Presence—He comes. This call of God upon the nation of Israel was to leave Egypt in order to worship. They were becoming a people who would be known by the Presence of God. He would become the distinguishing factor.

God's heart was for His entire nation of Israel to become priests. In fact, He commanded Moses to tell Israel of His desire. *"And you shall be to Me a kingdom of priests and a holy nation"* (Exod. 19:6). Priests minister to God. The plan of God having a people of His Presence was well underway. *Though Conditional on their obedience.*

Worship is powerful for many reasons. One of the most important is that we always become like the One we worship. This by itself would take Israel to new levels. But this call of God upon the nation of God would not go unnoticed.

The devil is very afraid of a worshiping people. He actually doesn't mind complacent worship, as it seems to work opposite to the real thing—it deadens our sensitivities to the Holy Spirit of God. It works completely opposite to the effects of sold out, passionate worship. Complacent worship is an oxymoron.

Satan's strategy against God's people and their call as God's intimates has never been clearer than when he revealed his hand through Pharaoh's words:

Go, sacrifice to your God within the land (Exodus 8:25).

Convenience and sacrifice cannot coexist. The *going* is a sacrifice, and a non-sacrificial people are of no consequence to the devil. The enemy knows there's power in the offering and will do whatever he can to distract us from giving it. Sometimes we fail to reach our destiny because we insist on it happening where we are—within reason, with little effort involved on our end. We often cannot get to a new place in worship until we get to a new place in God. I've heard so many people say through the years, "If it is God's will to move powerfully in my life (or church) He knows we're hungry, and He knows where we are." Foolishness! He's not a cosmic bellhop, bouncing around the universe to fulfill our every wish. He has a plan. And we must move into His plan. Wise men still travel, both in the natural and figuratively speaking.

I will let you go...only you shall not go very far away (Exodus 8:28).

The fear of fanaticism has kept many believers from their destiny. The only way to follow the One who died on the Cross in our place is to mirror His devotion! The Extreme One is calling out to extreme ones to come and follow Him. It is with that group He will change the world. Deep still calls to deep—the deep of God is still looking for people who have a similar depth in their hearts to respond equally to Him (see Ps. 42:7). Wasn't it the one with no depth in himself that Jesus warned us of in the parable of the seed and the sower? *"...Yet he has no firm root in himself, but is only temporary, and when affliction or persecution arises because of the word, immediately he falls away"* (Matt. 13:21).

Go now, you who are men, and serve the Lord (Exodus 10:11 NKJV).

Nothing is as fierce an opponent to the powers of darkness as the unified offering to God from multiple generations. This is one of the places where we see the mystery of compound interest in effect in the things of the Spirit. The fact that the devil puts so much effort into dividing the family unit and splintering the generations should testify to us of its importance. It has become all too common for one member of the family to stand out as the spiritual one, while the rest of the family is known for com-placency. Tragically, the spiritual one often gets exalted in pride, which brings division, or they lower the standard of their passion to fit the lowest common denominator in the family. Neither route is effective.

"Who Am I?"

Burn with passion no matter what, but maintain humility, being the servant of all. The momentum gained through the generations working together creates a spiritual wealth that truly makes nothing impossible for those who believe.[1] Even the unity *outside* of Christ is powerful. Consider Babel.

> *They said, "Come, let us build for ourselves a city, and a tower whose top **will reach** into heaven...." Lord said, "Behold, they are one people...and now nothing which they purpose to do will be impossible for them"* (Genesis 11:4,6).

When we add the supernatural power of the resurrected Christ to a people unified to His purpose and one another, *nothing* they purpose to do will be impossible for them.

> *Go, serve the Lord; only let your flocks and your herds be kept back. Let your little ones also go with you* (Exodus 10:24 NKJV).

This verse says a lot. At this point the devil was even willing to give up his immediate plan to influence and control their children if he could still manage their money. The New Testament unveils the power of this issue, saying *greed is idolatry* (see Col. 3:5). What kind of offering of importance can I possibly give to God that doesn't include my money or possessions? Nothing impressive. The offering from convenience protects form, ritual, and image. None of these things threaten the devil. He'll even attend the meetings where such priorities exist. And strangely, he'll go unnoticed. True worship involves my whole being. It is physical, emotional, spiritual, intellectual, and financial. It involves my relationships and my family, and it has a major impact on the boundaries I've set for how I want to live. Worship has a complete focus—God and His worth. It really is all about Him. It's about Presence. Israel, a generation of slaves at this point, was called to greatness. And their first step into such greatness was to worship Him extravagantly!

Go, serve the Lord as you have said (Exodus 12:31 NKJV).

Every plague, every act of violence and opposition to the enemies of God are simply God sparing no expense to preserve what is important to Him—an intimate people who worship. Mike Bickle says it best *all of God's judgments are aimed at that which interferes with love.* But this part of the story doesn't end here. We've seen that people are called to put everything on the line as they seek to follow God as worshipers. Just a few verses later we see how God rewarded them. *"And the Lord had given the people favor...thus* **they plundered the Egyptians"** (Exod. 12:36). Just when you think you gave up everything to follow God, He gives you more to offer.

The Water Rises Higher

Israel's journey is wild and long. And they finally make it into His land of promises. But it is the life of Moses I want us to learn from first. He was to become the example of something a nation could enter into. To emphasize this point he even describes his prophetic anointing as something that should be for everyone. *"Would that all the Lord's people were prophets, that the Lord would put His Spirit upon them!"* (Num. 11:29). Moses was a prototype in that he modeled a lifestyle that was above the Law. Not in the sense that the Law didn't apply to him. But he was above the Law in the sense that he had access to the presence of God in a way that was forbidden by the Law, even for the tribe of priests, the Levites. As such there's a part of Moses' lifestyle that gives a prophetic picture of what would be possible under the new covenant that was yet to come.

As I look at Israel's journey and the experiences with God from the many leaders in the Old Testament, Exodus 33 is the Bible's standout chapter in my perspective. Moses had several face-to-face encounters with God. But only one time that he came down from his meeting with God on the mountain did his face shine with the Presence of God. He literally radiated God's Presence (see Exod. 34:30). Not until Jesus, on the Mount of Transfiguration, would we see that phenomenon again (see Matt. 17:2). (But with Jesus, even His clothes shone with God's glory.)

There was one significant difference in the outcome of this encounter with God. This is the time he asked to see the glory of God, and God let all His goodness pass before his eyes (see Exod. 33:19). The outcome was that Moses' face shone because of seeing God's goodness. A revelation of God's goodness will change our countenance. God wants to change the face of His Church once again through a revelation of His goodness. He longs to raise up a people who will not just carry good news in the form of words. He longs to raise up a people who carry the good news in power, which is a Person (see 1 Cor. 4:20). It's Presence.

We must expect superior things from a superior covenant.

*But if the ministry of death, in letters engraved on stones, came with glory, so that the sons of Israel could not look intently at the face of **Moses** because of **the glory of his face**, fading as it was, **how will the ministry of the Spirit fail to be even more with glory?** (2 Corinthians 3:7-8)*

We must expect and press in for more!

The Ultimate Reputation

How do you want people to remember you? People work so hard to create an image and form a reputation for themselves. For some it's their beauty or their skills. For others it's their significance or their place in society. And still others work hard to create an image from the spiritual gifts they operate in. The Bible even teaches us the value of a good name (see Prov. 22:1). It is obviously important if it's done correctly. But if you could choose one thing to be known for, one thing that would distinguish you from everyone else, what would it be?

God chose Israel's reputation for them. At least He chose what He wanted it to be. They were the least of all, the most insignificant of all, the weakest of all nations. There was nothing about their natural qualities that made them stand out from any other people group. But there was this one thing that was to set them apart. *"And He said, 'My presence shall go with you, and I will give you rest'"* (Exod. 33:14). It would actually be the glory of God—His manifested Presence—that would be their distinguishing mark.

> *For how then can it be known that I have found favor in Your sight, I and Your people? Is it not by **Your going with us**, so that we, I and Your people, may be **distinguished from all the other people** who are upon the face of the earth?* (Exodus 33:16)

They would be distinguished from all other peoples by the Presence of God.

Favored Favorites

Church history is filled with people who obtained favor from the Lord in unusual ways. Most of us have favorites—those we have admired for various reasons, many according to our own history and background. These heroes of the faith reached places in God that we long for. Their place of great breakthrough is always to become the new norm as their example welcomes us to pursue Him in the same fashion. He still welcomes all.

In light of the subject of this chapter, one of those I admire most is Kathryn Kuhlman. I actually had the privilege to see her on several occasions as a young man. I respect her so much, for so many reasons. The miracles that came forth in her meetings are certainly one of the reasons. But let's lay that aside for a moment. Without being disrespectful, I'd like to tell you what she wasn't. She wasn't known as a great Bible teacher, or a great preacher, although she could do both. She didn't have natural beauty that seems to exalt others to a place of favor with man ahead of their appointed time. She wasn't a great singer, moving crowds with an amazing voice. And the list goes on. What could she do? She just seemed to be the person that God liked to be with. She is known for the Presence. The miracles came from that one thing. The mass conversions came from that one thing. The high places of worship that were experienced in her meetings came from that one thing. She was a Presence woman.

I still get teary-eyed when I watch the video where she talks about her point of absolute surrender to the Holy Spirit. It is a sobering moment indeed. She testifies of the precise moment, the precise location where she said the ultimate yes to God. Those moments don't reveal our strength. They actually reveal our weaknesses. To be all we can be requires that we are more dependent on God. If ever I saw a person who knew their need for absolute dependency on God it was Kathryn. She said yes and was given the privilege of hosting Him in ways that few have ever imagined.

One of the things she succeeded at, that so many of us miss in our lives, is that she knew who she wasn't. So many try to wear Saul's armor—in an attempt to operate in someone else's gift.[2] We see a person we admire and often jealously try to become them or surpass them. *Anyone who knows who God made them to be will never try to be someone else.* Kathryn illustrated this. But not only that, she illustrated it for the ultimate reason: She was known for *God being with her.*

The Inferior Points to the Future

Moses' life stands today as an invitation for all to enter a deeper place with God. The amazing part is that all that Moses experienced happened under an inferior covenant. His accomplishments and experiences should be held in high esteem by the Church. It would be foolish to do otherwise. But it would be equally foolish to ignore the fact that the high-water mark of the Old Testament was not to remain the high-water mark for the New. It is improper to expect superior blessings from an inferior covenant. Our New Testament heroes of the faith understood this. It gave them permission to press in for more.

The death of Christ satisfied the requirements of the Old Covenant while igniting the fires of the New. *"This cup is the new covenant in My blood; do this, as often as you drink it, in remembrance of Me"* (1 Cor. 11:25). When Jesus died, He paved the way for people to come directly into the Presence of God daily. This was unheard of in Moses' day. Only the high priest could do that, and it happened only one day a year—the Day of Atonement. The blood made it possible to be *a people of His Presence.* Certainly this possibility is much more available to us than it was to Israel under the Old Covenant. But the life-altering factor is this: Jesus' death made it possible to not only come into the Presence of God daily, but for the Presence of God to come into us permanently. We have become the eternal dwelling place of God (see Eph. 2:22). Incomprehensible!

Missing Pieces

"The fool has said in his heart, 'There is no God'" (Ps. 14:1). Even so, *many* question His existence, and His nature is questioned by *most* of the rest. Knowing the nature of faith and the

tension in this dilemma, the writer of Hebrews said, *"He who comes to God must believe that He is, and that He is the rewarder of those who diligently seek Him"* (Heb. 11:6). Confidence in His existence *and His nature* are the essentials to active faith. Faith thrives when we get those two issues settled. And it's not just a knowing He exists, somewhere out there. It's a knowing He is present, here and now. This kind of knowing is revealed by our response—*diligently seeking Him*. It's that kind of confidence in God. Understanding His nature sets the parameters for our faith. And those parameters are good and broad.

Moses had a series of life-altering encounters with God. The most notable was when he saw the fullness of God's goodness. There is no greater vacuum in the hearts and minds of humankind than understanding God's nature, especially as it pertains to the goodness of God. It seems that you can't even talk about the extreme kindness of God without someone voicing the concern for "sloppy agape" as they used to say, or an anything goes kind of Christianity. Unfortunately, the fear of exaggerating His goodness has kept many a heart from the liberty that He purchased on their behalf. It's not a rumor; He really is good, always good. And discovering His goodness gives me the grace to serve Him with reckless abandon.

It's hard to imagine that anyone would not want to surrender to this God of perfect goodness. Considering that even the Church struggles with this picture, it shouldn't surprise us that the unbeliever does. They'll need more than words. This one will have to come with Presence.

God is referred to as *"the Desire of All Nations"* (Hag. 2:7). That tells me that everyone wants a king like Jesus. He is what everyone longs for, yet has come to doubt even exists. The Church represents Jesus, which basically means to re-present Him. If we can host Him, and in the process become like Him, then perhaps the world will actually experience "it's My kindness that leads you to repentance" (see Rom. 2:4). They will be able to say, "I've tasted and seen that the Lord is good!" (See Psalms 34:8.)

ENDNOTES

1. Read *Momentum: What God Starts Never Ends* by Eric Johnson and Bill Johnson for more on this subject. It is also published by Destiny Image Publishers.

2. King Saul tried to get David to wear his own armor when he allowed him to fight Goliath. Saul was a large man. The armor didn't fit (see 1 Sam. 17:38-39). This represents the times we are tempted to fit into another person's assignment or gifting to carry out God's will for our lives. It doesn't work.

4

A PRESENCE
THAT EMPOWERS

The most feared and respected people in the Old Testament were the prophets. When they spoke, things happened. Their interactions with God produced a very healthy fear of God that often had a great impact on how people thought and lived. There was one thing that separated them from the rest of the crowd. It was that *the Spirit of the Lord came upon them*. Everything changed in that moment. They went from a respected citizen of a city to a feared citizen of Heaven. There's no doubt they had a *gift* from God that was unusual. They could *see*. Yet it was *the Spirit of God upon them* that had the most overwhelming influence. God spoke through them, backing His word with signs and wonders. These unusual people brought about some of history's most bizarre moments. And we are richer because of them.

The prophets were the most feared because the Spirit of the Lord came upon them. That's it. The Spirit of God, One who, Himself, saturates Heaven with His Presence, rests upon people. And when He does, things happen. These early prophets carried the Presence of God in a way that was rare, especially for their day. Their role is still often misunderstood in ours. They played a vital role in the increasing revelation of the interaction of God's abiding Presence and the purpose of man on earth. If we can see their history clearly and recognize the momentum created by these great men and women of God, we will be positioned to more readily embrace the assignment for our day. Ours is to be a greater day just as God has promised: *"The latter glory of this house will be greater than the former"* (Hag. 2:9). Plus, we are to have the benefit of greater clarity of heart and mind through advances that previous generations have obtained for us.

So many of these stories give us prophetic glimpses into a coming day—a day when what was bizarre and odd would become normal. Even now there are things we live with in the church that were once thought rare or impossible. Believe it or not, things are moving forward, progressing.

There is an obvious progression in the revelation of God for His people and an increase in His manifest Presence and glory. He meant it when He said, *"Of the increase of His government and of peace there will be no end"* (Isa. 9:7 NKJV). There has only been increase since those words were spoken. We have to adjust how we think and see to not only realize it but cooperate with what God is doing. Again it says of us, *"But the path of the righteous is like the light of dawn, that shines brighter and brighter until the full day"* (Prov. 4:18). We should and must expect progress. That same verse is even more fun in the Amplified.

But the path of the [uncompromisingly] just and righteous is like the light of dawn, that shines more and more (brighter and clearer) until [it reaches its full strength and glory in] the perfect day [to be prepared].

Expecting anything less than progression is to think against the true impact of the increasing manifestation of God's righteousness on the earth through His people.

Sovereignly His

Most of the time when the Spirit of God comes upon a person, He moves through them according to their own maturity and willingness to be used. I said most of the time. I have seen several occasions when the Spirit of God came upon someone and they weren't hungry, and in some cases they weren't even willing to be used. As a bystander, it put the fear of God in me. It was God acting in His sovereignty. Amazing, fearful, and wonderful, all at the same time.

Cal Pierce, the director of the Healing Rooms ministry based in Spokane, Washington, experienced one of those times. I saw God choose Him. If I were to live on this earth for another 1,000 years, I could never forget what I witnessed that night. God possessed a man.

My wife and I had been invited to become the new pastors of Bethel Church in Redding, California. The leadership heard what was happening in the church we were pastoring in Weaverville, California, and they were hungry for that at Bethel. Soon after we arrived, the outpouring of the Spirit began. It was wonderful, glorious, and controversial. It always is. Part of the church quickly opened their arms to this outpouring. Others left. Things were happening so quickly that the staff and leadership were unable to help lead in a way that was needed. At the suggestion of one of my pastoral staff members, we called for a private meeting just for the staff. They wanted to help me lead the church in this movement. In that meeting we had teams of people ready to serve the pastoral team and bring them into this divine encounter that was changing so many lives. It was beautiful. I scheduled the same for our leadership.

Somewhere around one hundred people gathered that night. I shared briefly what God was doing and invited the Holy Spirit to come. It was wonderful and simple. Cal and Michelle Pierce were a part of that team as Cal served on the church board. I found out later that they didn't like what was happening in the church and were putting their plans together to leave Bethel, the church they had been committed to for over 25 years. The controversy and the unusual manifestations of God quickly cooled their hearts for it all. Yet on this night, God had something else in mind. I watched God fall upon Cal and possess him. I wish I knew of another way to put it, but it wouldn't be honest. He became possessed by God, chosen for something that he wasn't even interested in. After almost everyone else had left the room, Cal was still standing, trembling, with waves of glory and power pulsating through and through his body. It was wonderful. It was glorious. It was sobering, really sobering. God had chosen His man. And the fruit that now flows from Cal and Michelle testifies to the impact of that moment, which can only be measured in eternity.

I have felt for a long time that too many things get swept under the carpet called the Sovereignty of God. In other words, He gets blamed for whatever happens. People often assume everything that happens must be His will because He is God. They call it *His sovereign will.* That simply isn't true. God is *"not wishing for any to perish but for all to come to repentance"* (2 Peter 3:9). Is anyone perishing? Yes. Is it God's will? No. Because of that, I tend to emphasize the role that we play in the outcome of things. Yet I love it when He violates my understanding and comfort zone and does something so incredibly sovereign that I stand with increased fear of Him. I've learned He will not violate His Word. But He doesn't seem to mind violating our understanding of His Word.

Un-willfully Prophetic

I once went to speak at a YWAM base in Colorado. Kris Vallotton, a businessman at the time, came with me to help. (He is now a very seasoned prophet on an international level who works on our staff at Bethel.) We watched the Spirit of God come upon many people in very wonderful ways. But He rested uniquely and powerfully upon a young lady who had no background in spiritual gifts, especially the prophetic. In fact, she didn't even believe they existed. God came upon her in ways that startled everyone. He wanted to speak through her. To be honest, I can't even say she was willing. She had no clue what was happening to and through her until it was over. It was so glorious, yet so sobering. The word of the Lord through her was powerful and pure. Her extremely conservative background had kept her pure from many of the things that contaminate that generation. We walked her around the room to pray for people (the anointing for this was obviously on her, not us). Each person we took her to was powerfully touched by the Lord through her words. Each prophetic word was so profound. She spoke of things she couldn't have known in the natural. Was it wonderful? Yes. Glorious? Yes, even beyond words. But Kris and I spent much time ministering to her between sessions because it scared her. And rightfully so. We knew it was God. But it was also beyond our norm.

This situation reveals such a great need for a culture that has an understanding of how the Spirit of God moves. So many people have no one to go to when God touches them in an unusual way. The common response with many in the church is to try to stay average, so our experience in God gets dumbed down to the lowest common denominator. People often, unknowingly, turn away from the anointing in their life to preserve their sense of control. The other extreme is they sometimes think they're going crazy because their experience seems so different from everyone else's. The enemy works to isolate us, and that's one of his tricks. We then end up sabotaging what God is actually doing. People in this position need help to process and learn of the gift that is in them.

Kris' personal story is quite profound. It took him years to discover what God was doing in him because it was so outside the box of our history and experience. If we had had more seasoned people around in the early days of his development, we could have shaved off years of turmoil for him. It's the reason he has such a heart for those with this unusual prophetic gift in their lives.

I know there are many who think this kind of encounter couldn't be God. After all, the Holy Spirit is a gentleman. At least that's what I was told throughout the wonderful years of the Charismatic Renewal of the '60s, '70s, and early '80s. A gentleman? My response is perhaps, but by His own definition of the word *gentleman*. Remember, this *Gentleman* knocked Saul of Tarsus off his donkey (see Acts 9). Read your Bibles. He does what He pleases. He is God and will not fit into our boxes.

There are many who are very much afraid that God would do such a thing to them and as a result fail to enter a place of total surrender. And then there's a whole other crowd that thinks if God would touch them that way, it would fix everything. God knows us inside out. He knows our greatest need and our greatest desire. As a perfect Father He longs to provide the very thing that is needed to take us to the next level. But He also knows what would distract us from our purpose and development. We must trust Him to arrange that part of our lives, while making sure that we hunger for and pursue all He makes available to us.

A King Gone Bad

Several Bible stories stand out in this regard. But I'll pick two because of their uniqueness. The first has to do with King Saul. He started as a good king. He had zeal for the Lord and rose up with righteous indignation when the enemies of Israel threatened the safety of His people. But he isn't remembered for that. He's remembered for his failures, as he eventually became a wicked king. A very wicked king.

Even though God knew what was in Saul's heart from the beginning, He gave him every opportunity to do well. At the start, Samuel the prophet told him about an encounter he would have that would change everything.

> *Afterward you will come to the hill of God where the Philistine garrison is; and it shall be as soon as you have come there to the city, that you will meet a **group of prophets** coming down from the high place with harp, tambourine, flute, and a lyre before them, and **they will be prophesying. Then the Spirit of the Lord will come upon you** mightily, and **you shall prophesy** with them and **be changed into another man*** (1 Samuel 10:5-6).

The Spirit of the Lord was already on the prophets. When Saul came into their atmosphere, what was on them got on him. I wish so much that we would learn to recognize when the Spirit of God is actually moving on someone else. Perhaps with honor we could learn how to avail ourselves of what He is doing in and through them so that we, too, would be impacted more intentionally by His Presence. The Spirit of God upon a person creates a heavenly atmosphere here and now. In this case, it was a group of prophets, so we have the exponential increase of Presence and power that can only come through unity. Two are better than one, if united. Two are less than one if divided. Learning to recognize this is essential for us to go where He has planned. It is called a *corporate anointing*.

This encounter was to set him up to be the kind of king Israel needed. When the Spirit of God came upon him, he was changed into another man. This encounter truly changed everything about him. It was up to him to "tend the new garden" that God had planted in his heart. We always have a role in our development. Gifts are free; maturity is expensive. *"It shall be when these signs come to you, do for yourself what the occasion requires, for God is with you"* (1 Sam. 10:7). This Holy Spirit realm would be necessary for him to accomplish what God intended as he led Israel to both safety and peace. Through these means, he would have access to the realms in God to *do what the occasion required*.

A Good Beginning

The prophetic encounter happened just as Samuel said it would. And it enabled Saul to start well. He had a much-needed sense of humility as well as a significant zeal for the name of the Lord. This encounter with the prophets no doubt changed him into the man that God needed in that position. But God is not responsible for our potential. We are. All of Heaven has been assigned to make sure we have everything we need to reach our God-designed destinies. The word of the Lord has been spoken. And we must act.

Through a series of disastrous choices, Saul becomes the untrustworthy king of Israel. God began to look for another one, one after His heart. He found a young man tending his father's sheep. He was a worshiper. His name was David.

One of the most frightening statements one could possibly hear is, *"Now the Spirit of the Lord departed from Saul"* (1 Sam. 16:14). The great gift and the great responsibility has everything to do with His Presence. Later in David's own life we hear him cry,

"Do not take your Holy Spirit from me" (Ps. 51:11). The Presence of God must be our prize!

The Wicked Gets Anointed

Here is a very strange part of the story. It is years later and Saul is now a very wicked king. He hates the anointing and especially hates the anointed one—David. It became obvious to him that God had chosen another man to serve as king because Saul had abused his position. Saul was jealous of David and tried to kill him. So he sent servants to capture David so he could get rid of the one who reminded him of what he had lost.

> *Then **Saul sent messengers to take David**, but when they saw the company of the prophets prophesying, with Samuel standing and presiding over them, **the Spirit of God came upon the messengers of Saul; and they also prophesied.** When it was told Saul, **he sent other messengers, and they also prophesied.** So **Saul sent messengers again the third time, and they also prophesied.** Then **he himself went** to Ramah and came as far as the large well that is in Secu; and he asked and said, "Where are Samuel and David?" And someone said, "Behold, they are at Naioth in Ramah." He proceeded there to Naioth in Ramah; and **the Spirit of God came upon him also, so that he went along prophesying continually** until he came to Naioth in Ramah. He also stripped off his clothes, and **he too prophesied before Samuel** and lay down naked all that day and all that night. Therefore they say, "Is Saul also among the prophets?"* (1 Samuel 19:20-24)

When the Spirit of God comes upon people, they do extraordinary things in His name. The Spirit of God coming upon a group of people automatically charges the atmosphere. It happened in this story. The prophets are prophesying, and the air is thick with the Presence of God. And the servants with a murderous assignment fall under the influence of the prophetic and begin to function outside of their gifting. They prophesied. He sent a second group, who responded to the anointing in the same way. And finally, he sent a third with the exact same outcome. That had to frustrate Saul to no end. He knew what was happening to them. He knew because that was in his history. He had had the same experience. That's probably why he didn't kill these servants who failed at their assignment.

A Glimpse of Grace

This is such an amazing picture of grace. It's why I say there are many instances in the Old Testament that are actually pictures of New Testament realities. And this is one. Grace is most often defined as *unmerited favor*. And that's the perfect place to start in defining this significant word. But a more complete definition is, it's the *unmerited favor that brings His enabling Presence*. Here was the enabling presence of God giving people a chance to taste of life in its fullness. Certainly this gave Saul's servants a chance to rethink how they wanted to live their lives. They'd tasted of life in the Spirit. Hopefully they were now ruined for anything else. This is a prophetic glimpse of grace.

Saul finally decides to go himself. And even though he is in such a horrible condition, with a heart filled with wickedness, he comes into the atmosphere of the manifest Presence of God upon the prophets and *prophesies continually*. The weirdest part of the story is that he took off all of his clothes. I'm sure there's great spiritual significance to that part of the story that I'm missing. But I know this much—he's returning, even if for a short while, to a previous place of humility. Plus, without any clothes on, you probably won't be going anywhere real soon. He seems to be saying, "I'm vulnerable before the prophet Samuel. And I'm not going anywhere!" Again he had the opportunity for transformation because of the anointing. Saul encountered the Holy Spirit—the anointing that sets free. *"The yoke shall be destroyed because of the anointing"* (Isa. 10:27 KJV). But it didn't stick. You can have a perfectly planted garden. But without continual maintenance, the garden will become a garden of weeds in no time at all.

We must steward the life that God gives us. *"From everyone who has been given much, much will be required"* (Luke 12:48). King Solomon experienced disaster in his own life because he failed at this one thing. God gave him more than anyone to ever live. The one verse about him that pierces my heart more than any other is, *"Now the Lord was angry with Solomon because his heart was turned away from the Lord, the God of Israel, **who had appeared to him twice**"* (1 Kings 11:9). God gave Solomon the most unusual encounters with Him, twice, but their effect didn't last. We are accountable for what we've been given. It is up to us to keep the impact of an old experience current.

I've seen people receive a dramatic touch from the Lord. And when they don't steward that touch, things go sour in their lives. Critics of revival tend to want to discount the touch of God and say, "See, I told you, that wasn't really God's touch on his life in the first place." Should God be questioned because of man? Jesus talked about healing ten lepers. Only one returned to give thanks (see Luke 17:15-18). Does that mean that the other nine didn't really receive a touch from God? Of course not. The validity of God's work is never determined by man's response, good or bad. His work is measured by this: They had leprosy, and now they don't. Or, "I once was blind, but now I see" (see John 9:25). Or the person touched by God was healed of cancer. The doctor verified it. We give God all the praise.

What really causes people to stumble is if that person gets cancer or another disease again. Too often people assume God brought it back because it was His will in the first place. God didn't cause it to come back any more than He gave it in the first place.

You can't have Jesus healing a disease that the Father purposed for the person to have or you have a divided house—one that will not stand (see Luke 11:17). This brings up another issue for another day. But the lack is never on God's end of the equation. It would be foolish to question God because of a lack that squarely rests on the shoulders of people. (The issue of reoccurring diseases is a serious one and must be addressed, *without* giving God the credit for the devil's work. Reading Luke 11:24-26 and First Corinthians 11:27-30 is a good place to start.)

A Fearful Warrior

The second story actually provides an insight to the ways of the Spirit that is actually my favorite in the entire Bible. This one is about one of the judges of Israel: Gideon.

Gideon is an individual who quickly becomes a favorite for many in the same way as the apostle Peter because we find it easy to identify with him. He was fearful, plain and simple. When God was looking for someone to deliver Israel from their oppressor, He chose Gideon. There's no obvious reason, at least not one that stands out to me.

God found Gideon hiding in a winepress, trying to thresh wheat. The Midianites had been stealing from the children of Israel for quite a while. He no doubt was trying to get some provisions for his family without being robbed again. Regardless, threshing wheat in a winepress provides a fascinating picture. Wheat speaks of the *bread of the Word*—teaching. Wine represents the *felt experience of the Holy Spirit*—sometimes intoxicating encounters. They are never in conflict with each other from God's perspective. But they often are in ours. Each serves a purpose that the other can't address. The interesting picture is of Gideon trying to get the bread of His Word out of a place where wine is made. It won't work.

We saw this in the early days of the outpouring. People were angry because there wasn't as great an emphasis on teaching. We tried. It's just tough to get bread out of grapes. Most every time we did, we seemed to be working against God's heart for the moment. The opposite is also true. Many just want to sit around and sing or laugh when God wants to build our understanding through His Word. My philosophy is this: When God is serving wine, drink. When He's serving bread, eat.

The Mighty Are Hiding

God speaks through the angel of the Lord and calls Gideon a mighty man of valor (see Judg. 6:12). Gideon responds, *"O my lord, if the Lord is with us, why then has all this happened to us? And where are all His miracles which our fathers told us about?"* (Judg. 6:13). This seems so funny to me. An angel just spoke to him while he's hiding in a winepress, and almost without missing a beat he has a response to the angel. It shouldn't surprise us to know what Gideon was thinking about when the angel showed up. His guns were loaded.

If there was any verse in the Bible that seemed to describe the heart of people who often miss out on what God is doing, it's this one: *If God is with us, why has all this bad stuff happened? And where are the miracles we have always heard about?* To this day most don't seem to realize that He doesn't cause the bad stuff, but instead equips us with the authority, power, and assignment to deal with the devil and his works. It is up to us to learn how to use the tools God gives us. If we don't, the devil continues to steal. To Gideon's credit, he responds to the word of the Lord and offers a sacrifice to God.

Once again a story needs to be abbreviated for the sake of space. The bottom line of this story is that Gideon is afraid at the beginning. He's afraid in the middle of the story. I'm sure that when God reduced his army from 32,000 men down to 300, it didn't help.

Finally, God gives him confirmation that He is with him and then releases his assignment to Gideon. And just to fit into God's unique way of doing things, he told Gideon what to do if he was afraid.

> *Now the same night it came about that the Lord said to him, "Arise, go down against the camp, for I have given it into your hands. But **if you are afraid** to go down, **go with Purah your servant down to the camp,** and you will hear what they say; and afterward your hands will be strengthened that you may go down against the camp." **So he went with Purah his servant down to the outposts of the army that was in the camp*** (Judges 7:9-11).

Notice the Lord said, "If you're afraid, go down to the camp of the Midianites." The next phrase says he went down to the camp. Again, that tells us he's still dealing with fear. Plus, the enemy's camp is a strange place to go to get encouragement. Moses once sent 12 spies out to get a good look at the Promised Land, which also happened to be an enemy's land. Ten spies brought back a bad report because of their fear and made the nation of Israel afraid (see Num. 13:25-33). Those ten spies just stayed together and fed one another's fears.

Sometimes the best place to go to get encouraged is the enemy's camp. That's where the two spies got their encouragement, and they refused to allow the fearful ten to feed them their fear. And now this is where God sent Gideon, the fearful one. It almost seems like divine humor—if you're afraid, go to the one you're afraid of. As he did, he heard that one of them had a dream, which the other interpreted as being about Gideon wiping them out (see Judg. 7:13-14). That indeed encouraged him.

The Ultimate Picture

The story goes on to report that Gideon and his men did exactly that. They beat the Midianites and restored Israel to a place of strength and out from under the abuse of surrounding nations. It's a wonderful story. But in the middle of this miracle is a most unusual verse. *"So the Spirit of the Lord came upon Gideon"* (Judg. 6:34). That would be good enough just as it is. But it really says so much more. The word "came upon" actually means *to put on, wear, clothe, be clothed.*[1] In the footnotes of my study Bible[2] it says, "In Hebrew this literally means 'The Spirit of the Lord clothed Himself with Gideon.'" Stunning! God is clothed with Gideon. I can't think of any picture of the Spirit-filled life that more accurately describes my heart more than this one: God put Gideon on like a glove.

Here is the picture: The Presence of God is hosted by a person so significantly that He actually lives through them. It's not cancelling out who they are. It's capturing it to the fullest, immersed in divine influence. It is as though their personality, their gifts and demeanor are all being expressed through God living in them. Most importantly, here is another grace moment. Gideon had received *favor that brought the enabling Presence of God into His life to empower him* to do what was impossible for him to do.

From some, this would imply that it's all Jesus and none of us. I don't believe that. There's no question that He is the determining factor in any significant situation. But we sometimes get an unhealthy view of our lives and our own place in His plan. I've heard so many pray, "None of me, all of You!" It's a noble prayer. I'm sure it comes out of a desire to not have our selfishness exert any influence on the outcome of things. But shouldn't our righteousness have an effect on the outcome of things if He has in fact made us so? God had none of us before we were created. He didn't like it. That's why He made us.

It's not as though we don't matter and only Jesus matters. Many take John the Baptist's prayer as a model, *"He must increase, but I must decrease"* (John 3:30). That is actually not a legal prayer for us. John was closing out a season as the greatest Old Testament prophet. He was passing the baton on to Jesus who would initiate the existence of the Kingdom of God on earth. The focus was shifting from *John and the Law* to *Jesus and the Kingdom.* John had to decrease. Jesus had to increase. But when Jesus left the earth He didn't say we were to decrease. Instead He passed that same baton on to us with His name, power, and authority and commissioned us to continue in what He started. *"As the Father has sent me, I also send you"* (John 20:21). What is needed is not less of us and more of Him. What is needed is *all of us covered and filled by all of Him!*

There's no question Jesus is the answer. But He won't do it without us. That has been His plan from the beginning. So we need to think consistently with His ways, pray according to His promises, and live according to His provision and *be put on like a glove again.*

Selah

The lessons we glean from Saul's story aren't about Saul at all. Neither is the Gideon story really about Gideon. In each case we are looking at the privilege to host the Spirit of God, the great prize, and learn how He moves and works in and through people. This is the one assignment we were all born for.

ENDNOTES

1. From the New American Standard Exhaustive Concordance.

2. *The Spirit-Filled Life Bible*, page 357.

5

SNEAK PREVIEWS

God, the master Producer and Orchestrator of life, has some surprises in store for us all. He just loves to tell secrets to His own. And throughout history, He has given glimpses of what was to come.

Because of the Master's design, everyone lives to make life better. Some serve the betterment of humankind, and others merely serve themselves. But as people, we carry a sense of hope that things can and must be better than they presently are. This affects all areas of life—science, technology, entertainment, etc. Everything lives under the influence of this inner desire. It is in the nature of humans, the result of being made in the image of God. This is the way creative people function. We draw upon God-given abilities to come up with solutions to solve problems and answer whatever issue is in the way of progress.

God works with this instinct and draws us into our potential through promise and the wonder of possibility. Because of this, we live in the tension between what is and what is to come. God has given every human being a sense of hope for a better future. Some drown out that inner conviction through sarcasm, the defense mechanism of disappointment, while others silence that voice by a theology of unbelief. Still others have it stolen from them through abusive treatment by others. But it was planted there in the beginning and can be restored.

God is famous for giving *sneak previews* to His coming attractions. While *"it is the glory of God to conceal a matter"* (Prov. 25:2), He loves to reveal things to His people. That's because He doesn't hide things *from* us. He hides things *for* us.[1] The Old Testament serves that purpose.

The Old Testament is filled with teachings and revelations that were for the practical expressions of life and worship for Israel. Yet ultimately they were things that prophesied of and spoke to the future. It dealt with everything from the coming Messiah to the new nature given to His people to God's relationship to humankind. Each subject and promise was wonderful, but way beyond comprehension.

Seeing Beyond

The prophets were often called seers. The title wouldn't be necessary if all they saw was what already existed. The gift was to enable them to see the unseen of their day as well as to have a *knowing* of the coming days.

The New Covenant era is what the prophets looked ahead to see and spoke about. They pointed to this moment in time. They were serving Israel, for sure. But ultimately, they were serving both the *wild olive branch* as well as the *natural branch*—the Gentile and Jew who would make up that mysterious people called the Body of Christ (see Rom. 11:17-24; Eph. 3:4-9). They were serving those who would be alive in the last days, which started at the resurrection of Christ. And this is now 2,000 years later, the last of the last days.

Born to Dream

Make at least a mental list of the kings and prophets who are your heroes, the ones who actually dreamed of the day we live in: Solomon, David, Isaiah, and Daniel. The list goes on and on. And yet there's not one of them who saw what was coming and did not have an ache in their hearts to be able to taste of that reality—a reality that we now enjoy. The primary focus of their dream was twofold: 1) to have a new heart with a new nature, and 2) to have the Spirit of God live in and rest upon each believer. Those two ideas were beyond comprehension for everyone, even the 12 disciples. Jesus had to instruct them that the Holy Spirit being here with them would even be better than having Him, the Son of God, with them in the flesh (John 16:7). Yet there wasn't one of them that wouldn't have chosen to have Jesus remain in the flesh if the option had been given to them. Without knowing it, they were on the edge of something that had been the inner focus of many of the *greats* who had gone before them—a tipping point, as some would describe it.

> *For I say to you, that many prophets and kings wished to see the things which you see, and did not see them, and to hear the things which you hear, and did not hear them* (Luke 10:24).

Prophets and kings, the *who's who* of biblical days, had an awareness of a superior reality that was coming. And as much as they longed to be a part of it, it was forbidden. That privilege was reserved for you. Those great history-makers stand in the cloud of witnesses watching with both excitement and wonder as the mystery of Christ unfolds before their eyes. Of course, we did nothing to earn the privilege. It is the choice of the Sovereign One. Having said that, I recognize that it brings us to a deep place of responsibility and accountability because we have access to something that these kings and prophets missed out on. Sobering indeed.

Let's assume for a moment that Solomon is one of the kings of which Jesus spoke in the Luke 10 passage—a safe assumption, I think, considering the nature of his wisdom and his prophetic insights. Think about what it must have felt like for this uniquely privileged man to long for our day. He had all the possible wealth this world could offer, enough to make that of the wealthiest of this day pale in comparison. His impact on nations caused leaders who hated him to serve him. He was feared because of this wisdom that seemed to come with Presence, for wisdom is a person (see 1 Cor. 1:30). Enemies sat in silence because of it. Nations talked about him. Even kings and queens traveled great distances just to hear him speak. They would even try to trick him with life's most difficult questions, yet he would answer them all. His skeptics became fans. There was nothing he could dream of that he couldn't have. That is, except for one thing—the future.

Kings and prophets, the ones most mindful of unseen realities, were given sneak previews of what was coming. And every one of them would give anything they had to taste of what we have been given.

David was no doubt one of those referred to in this passage. He was both king and prophet. *"Brethren, I may confidently say to you regarding the patriarch David…because he was a prophet… he looked ahead and spoke"* (Acts 2:29-31). It's what prophets do. They see beyond their day and speak accordingly.

The king and the prophet is the apostle/prophet combination of the Old Testament. To imply that apostles are kings only works when we see kings by God's design—highly favored to serve more effectively—the least of all.

Hunger Increased

All of the face-to-face encounters were ahead of time in the sense that that level of intimacy was to become normal only after the blood of Jesus was shed. Even Gideon had to pinch himself to make sure he was still alive after his encounter with God (see Judg. 6:22-24). He seemed surprised to find out he actually was. The Old Testament is filled with people who got to taste of things ahead of time. Sneak previews.

Have you ever gone to see a movie because the advertisement made it look so funny, but when you saw it, you noticed all the funny moments in the movie were already in the trailer? It's a great disappointment. The movie never got any better than that 60-second spot. God is not like that. He entices and draws us into faith for the impossible, and then completely outdoes Himself. It's just the way He is. He gives a glimpse of something to come, knowing that even those who saw it coming would be surprised when it actually did. His coming works are represented in words and pictures, but can never be fully contained in them. He surpasses all description and everyone's anticipation of good. He is extreme in all the right ways.

We have been given one of the greatest privileges of all time—abound with hope in a time of hopelessness. That is a *light on a hill*. Even so, many who have been given the honor to steward hope have allowed the pressures of this life to derail them from their purpose. And the one who is to be a fountain of hope actually mirrors the hopelessness of those without Christ. This is especially true as it pertains to the last days. When they consider the future, they can only really get happy about the fact that Heaven is near. And they should. That is to be the great hope for every believer. But our assignment should concern us more than our destination. We must be known for hope for the day we live in, as the purposes of God are always great. He will do everything needed, according to His promises for His victorious bride. When Jesus said there would be *wars and rumors of wars*, He wasn't giving us a promise (see Matt. 24:6). He was describing the conditions into which He was releasing His last days army of transformational people.

Prophetic Snap Shots

Consider just a few things that they saw that told them of the *greater* that was coming. Besides the prophets' promises that the Messiah would come, the earth would be filled with His glory, and Israel would rise to a restored place of prominence, there were the experiences, the symbols, the types and shadows that all spoke of something coming that was greater. For example:

- They sacrificed sheep recognizing that a lamb was coming who would forever atone for sin. God would provide for Himself a Lamb.

- All the furniture of Moses' Tabernacle was laid out in the shape of a cross. They sacrificed at this Tabernacle when the cross was not even yet a form of corporal punishment.

- Each piece of furniture spoke of the Messiah, representing something distinct about the nature and function of Christ, i.e. table of showbread—Jesus the Bread of Life; candlestick—Jesus the Light of the World, etc.

- Abraham instinctively sought for a city whose builder and maker is God (see Heb. 11:9-10). That cry for the coming Kingdom came before there were any prophecies concerning it or even teachings from the rabbis.

- David learned something in the Presence of God that couldn't be taught from the Law—God really didn't want the sacrifice of bulls and goats. He longed for the sacrifice of the heart—brokenness and yieldedness (see Ps. 51:17).

- David found out that God inhabited praise (see Ps. 22:3 KJV).

- Only priests could carry God's presence. He wasn't to be put on ox carts or anything man made (see Exod. 25).

This list is endless in possibility, profound in its impact. God gave insights way ahead of time. When He shows us what's coming, it's not so we will strategize and plan. It's so we'll get hungry and draw into our day what was reserved for another day.

They had a sense that something was coming that was glorious beyond description. I do believe one of the primary works of the devil is to get us to discount the moment we live in. As long as we *idolize* another era we'll be blind to the importance of our own.

Past, Present, and Future

I was very active in sports, especially in my teen and early adult years. Whether it's baseball, tennis, or golf, a swing has three basic components. There is the backswing, the point of contact, and the follow-through. Disciplined and skilled athletes learn to be consistent in those three things. Metaphorically speaking, the backswing is our history while the point of contact is the moment we live in. The follow-through is the destiny/future according to promise.

Our backswing is God's personal history and accomplishments for us through Christ. We inherited His history as though it were ours all along. He took what we deserved so we could receive what He deserved. The point of contact is this moment we're in, realizing that God has a unique purpose for our lives. It's not only about the future. It's also about the moment we are in that is so magnificent, that only unbelief and introspection can rob me from its fullness. The follow-through is a future filled with hope because the history is so solid and secure. The follow-through is in the same arch as the backswing. In other words, when the backswing is right and the point of contact is right, the follow-through is predictable. One sets up the other. He has gone ahead of us, fully securing the future for us. Faithfulness keeps us in sync with His perfect plan. Whenever God gives us a promise, it's because He has gone into our future and brought back the word necessary to get us there.

Throughout the Bible, God is creating a desire within the hearts of His people not only for Heaven as a location, but Heaven as the realm of His present rule. (*Kingdom* is broken down into two words—*king's domain*.) It is right and good to long for Heaven as my home. But it is my responsibility to equally long for His rule here and now. God's job is to get me to Heaven. My job is not to go to Heaven; my job is to bring Heaven to earth through my prayers and obedience.

The House Is a Gate Is a House

One of my favorite pictures of the Church is found in the Old Testament story of Jacob in Genesis 28. Perhaps it's the abstract nature of the story that draws me to it. I'm not sure. But I know there is a promise of something so significant here that it will take a very special generation to draw it out completely.

Then Jacob departed from Beersheba and went toward Haran. He came to a certain place and spent the night *there, because the sun had set; and he took one of the stones of the place and put it under his head, and lay down in that place. He had a dream, and behold, a ladder was set on the earth with its top reaching to heaven; and behold, the angels of God were ascending and descending on it. ...Then Jacob awoke from his sleep and said, "Surely the Lord is in this place, and I did not know it." And he was afraid and said, "How awesome is this place! This is none other than **the house of God**, and **this is the gate of heaven."** ...He called the name of that place Bethel* (Genesis 28:10-12,16-17,19).

This is the first mention of the house of God in the Bible. One of the more meaningful principles of Bible interpretation is that the first mention of something in Scripture carries extra weight. It sets a standard for a subject that the rest of Scripture will support and add to. The rather strange part of this example of the house of God is that there is no building there. It's not a tabernacle or tent that is movable, neither is it a temple that is permanent. It is God with man on the side of a hill. It's a great picture of reality from God's perspective. It's the house of God.

The elements of this story are simple—open Heaven, Father's voice, angels ascending and descending, and ladder on the earth reaching to Heaven. This in its entirety is a picture of the church. But the most astonishing part is the conclusion Jacob made from this revelation. *This is none other than the house of God, the gate of Heaven.* Did you catch it? The house of God *is* the gate of Heaven.

Gates are simple but interesting items that are a part of our daily lives. Perhaps you have one that takes you from your front yard to the public sidewalk, or your backyard to the driveway. A gate is a transition place that takes you from one realm or place to another.

This picture is quite profound. The Church is the eternal dwelling place of God. And at this moment in time it is a building built on the edge of two worlds. We are dual citizens of both Heaven and earth. As such, we are not only those who are to pray for God's Kingdom to come, we are the tools who are often used by God to release that reality into this one. I'm not sure that we are to always know the magnitude of what we're doing or the impact we are having. But it's helpful to understand that our obedience always releases His world into this one in a way that is more substantial than we ever thought possible.

Surprising Instructions

God had revealed so much to the prophets, not only through their prophetic words, but also in their heavenly experiences. As stated, I believe it was written in the hearts of prophets as well as the average person that there was more, much more than had ever been considered possible. It's the nature of humanity to crave, dream, and desire. You can't crave for something sweet if something sweet doesn't exist. In the same way, the hunger for more in God testifies that more actually exists and is available. That's what drove Abraham to look for the unseen. *"He was looking for the city which has foundations, whose architect and builder is God"* (Heb. 11:10). It was the inner conviction that something substantial, more real, eternal, and built by God Himself is available for all.

Jesus spoke to His disciples in a very strange way. He said, *"In My Father's house are many dwelling places; **if it were not so, I would have told you;** for I go to prepare a place for you"* (John 14:2). You'd think He would be saying, *If it were so, I would tell you.* Or, *Because it is so, I have told you.* Why was His approach so opposite to our thinking? He had no need to promise them what they had an inner awareness of. He is speaking to an assumed awareness of heavenly realms that exists in the heart of every person. He is acknowledging that reality. His job would be to tell them that their inner awareness, their inner dream, was not true and had no basis in reality *if it were not so.*

Jesus is the Light that enlightens everyone who comes into the world. Everyone has received this enlightenment. But busyness, shame, and pride keep us from being in touch with the understanding of the unseen that God has put into the consciousness of every person born on this earth. What we do with this insight is up to us.

The Prophets' Prayer

I can only imagine the nature of the prophets' dreams. They not only had the inborn awareness of more, some of them had caught glimpses of what was coming. And some even saw Heaven, the throne of God, and the mysterious angelic realms. The overall hunger was for God's world to have an effect on this one. Isaiah even prayed, *"Rend the heavens and come down!"* (Isa. 64:1). It was a prophetic word in the form of a prayer. Anointed prayer always has a prophetic nature to it.

The cry for Heaven to influence earth had once again exploded from the heart. This time it was a prophet. God had already set the stage to answer this and instructed Isaiah to pray and declare it.

ENDNOTE

1. This concept is developed in my book, *Dreaming with God*, Chapter 10, starting with page 169.

6

ANSWERS TO
ANCIENT CRIES

The cries for God, some from the righteous and some from the unrighteous, have sounded through the ages. I grew up hearing there was a God-shaped vacuum in the heart of every person. I believe it.

This longing for God is seen in so many ways, including the drive to make things better in life. I've traveled all over the world. And one thing that exists in every people group I've seen is the desire to discover new things and make what exists better. This passion is firmly rooted in everyone.

God created us with desires and passions and the capacity to dream. All of these traits are necessary to truly make us like Him.

With these abilities, we can discover more of God, our purpose in life, and the beauty and fullness of His Kingdom. When these abilities exist unharnessed by divine purpose, they take us to forbidden fruit. It was a risk God was willing to take in order to end up with His dream—those made in His image, who worship Him by choice, who carry His Presence into all the earth.

Isaiah represented the cry of all humanity when he prayed, *"Rend the heavens and come down!"* It was known somehow that the realities of Heaven and earth must be closer to each other. In this prayer, the cry for Heaven to influence earth had once again exploded from the heart. This time it was from a prophet. God had already set the stage to answer and instructed Isaiah to make the prayerful declaration. It was a prophetic word in the form of a prayer.

Heaven's answer came. The revelation and release of God's redemptive program is now unstoppable.

Heaven is a Person

The water baptism of John was known as a baptism of repentance. That made Jesus' request of John to baptize Him strange and quite difficult to process. Jesus had no sin to repent of. But John's baptism was also a part of his announcement of the Kingdom being near. When John said the Kingdom was near, he was prophesying about what Jesus would manifest and release.

John knew he wasn't worthy to baptize Jesus. In fact, he confessed his need for the baptism that Jesus would bring—in the Holy Spirit and fire (see Matt. 3:11). But Jesus insisted. Being willing to do what you are not qualified to do is sometimes what qualifies you.

Jesus answered John's objection, *"Permit it at this time; for in this way it is fitting for us to fulfill all righteousness"* (Matt.

3:15). Righteousness was fulfilled in this act because here Jesus became the servant of all, identified with sinful humanity, and was now positioned to announce that the Kingdom of God is at hand. The announcement brought the release, as nothing happens in the Kingdom until first there is a declaration.

When Jesus was baptized in water, Heaven took notice. Here is an interesting description of this divine moment.

> *Immediately coming up out of the water, He saw the heavens opening, and the Spirit like a dove descending upon Him; and a voice came out of the heavens: "You are My beloved Son, in You I am well-pleased"* (Mark 1:10-11).

Jesus saw the *heavens opening*. What had been promised through the ages had started. But no one expected this: Heaven invading earth through the humility of a man—the Son of God, the Son of Man.

The word *opening* means to *cleave, split.* It is translated as *opening*, *split*, and *tears* one time each, *divided* and *tear* two times each, and *torn* four times. Interestingly, it is the same word used to describe both the veil in the temple being *torn* and the rocks *splitting* open at Jesus' death, as Heaven and earth shook as a witness to the injustice of that moment—One so perfect dying for those who deserve death. *"And behold, the veil of the temple was* **torn** *in two from top to bottom; and the earth shook and the rocks were* **split**" (Matt. 27:51). In other words, the *heavens opening* at Jesus' baptism by John was not a simple parting of the clouds. It was a violent act, first represented by Isaiah's language when he prayed **rend** *the heavens and* **come down** (Isa. 64:1). An invitation had been made on behalf of humanity, and God answered in person.

Tearing the heavens was in itself an act of ultimate grace and glory, resulting in spiritual forces of darkness suffering serious consequences. The Man, Christ Jesus, is now clothed with

Heaven, thoroughly equipped for all His earthly purposes. And His equipping was a prophetic foretaste of what would soon be made available to all.

Signs to Make You Wonder

The veil in the temple, the rocks around Jerusalem, and the heavens all experience the same act of violence. They give witness that the King with a superior Kingdom has just come onto the scene.

- *The veil*—God was not tied to an Old Covenant anymore as the requirements had been met through Jesus' death. It was torn top to bottom, as it was His doing.

- *The rocks*—the hardest places on earth were responding to the change in seasons, splitting open to signify that Jesus, the King of glory, was welcome to rule here.

- *The heavens*—the prince of the power of the air had no authority over Jesus, who would be the prototype of every believer who would walk the earth after His death, resurrection, and ascension into Heaven.

So then, what happened when the heavens were torn open in this act of violence? The Spirit of God came down. This is the answer to Isaiah's prayer. This is in response to the cries of the kings and prophets who all ached for this day. Jesus paved the way for His experience to become our experience. The Holy Spirit, the treasure of Heaven that Jesus and the Father spoke so reverently about, has been released on earth. To look for another open Heaven is to incorrectly steward the one we've been given.

Open Heavens

Every believer has an open Heaven. For the believer, most closed heavens are between the ears. Living as though the heavens were brass over us actually plays into the devil's hands as it puts us in a defensive posture. This violates what Jesus accomplished. He put us on offense with His commission, *"Go!"* Remember, believing a lie empowers the liar.

This certainly doesn't mean that darkness isn't able to cast a long shadow over a person, or even a city or a nation. We often find ourselves in spiritually dark environments. I can take you places where just being there could cause you to tremble, as the realm of darkness is so prevalent, destructive, and dominant. Even so, it is an inferior power, one I cannot afford to be impressed with. My attention must be on the provisions and promises of Christ and the open Heaven over me. I believe that keeping my focus on those things describes at least in part what it means to abide in Christ (see John 15:4). Plus, our refusal to fear reminds the devil that he is finished! (See Philippians 1:28.) If for some reason you can't seem to sense what to do in a given environment, worship. When in doubt, always worship.

We cannot let darkness shape our awareness of the heavenly atmosphere that dwells upon us. The *size* of the open heaven over us is affected in some measure by our maturity and yieldedness to the Holy Spirit. Think of the open Heaven as a big oak tree. The bigger and more stable the tree is, the more people can stand under its shade. Mature believers carry Heaven's atmosphere in such a way that others are able to stand under their shade and receive protection. To use another analogy, others can *draft* on our breakthroughs and become changed.

To live unaware of the open Heaven over us is to contribute to the war over our hearts and minds as it pertains to the truth of Scripture. Then we will always see what hasn't happened instead of living from what has happened. We owe it to God to live aware of what He has done and draw from the reality He has made available. Not doing so costs us dearly. The heavens were torn open, and there is no demonic power that is able to sew them back together. Besides, the Father longs for the Spirit who lives in us. What power of darkness exists that could block their fellowship? But when we live with a primary awareness of the enemy and his plans, we instinctively live in reaction to darkness. Again, if I do, then the enemy has had a role in influencing my agenda. And he isn't worthy. My life must be lived in response to what the Father is doing. That is the life Jesus modeled for us.

Heaven is filled with perfect confidence and peace, while this world is filled with chaos and mistrust in God. We always reflect the nature of the world we are most aware of. Living aware of open heavens has incalculable results.

Can God Come to Where He Is?

Some are bothered when we talk about God coming into a situation, His Spirit falling upon us, or the Holy Spirit moving in a meeting, etc. Often, as we get ready to minister to people, we will invite the Holy Spirit to come, in the John Wimber fashion. The question is, "Why invite God to come when He is already here?" It's a good question. It makes no sense whatsoever to pray that way unless we understanding that there are different measures and dimensions of God's Presence. When He is here, there is always more to come. It's important to hunger for and invite that increase. Isaiah had a perception of this reality, saying, *"I saw the Lord sitting on a throne, lofty and exalted, with the train of His robe filling the temple"* (Isa. 6:1). The word *filling* implies that His robe filled the temple, but then continued to fill it. He came, but He kept coming. There is always more!

This is at least a partial list of these measures of His Presence; each one is an increase of the previous:

- God first inhabits everything and holds all things together (see Col. 1:17). He is everywhere, the glue that holds His creation in place.

- A second dimension of God's Presence is His indwelling Holy Spirit in the lives of those who have been born again. He specifically comes to make us His tabernacle.

- A third dimension is seen when believers gather in His name. As He promised, He is *"there in their midst"* (Matt. 18:20). This is where the principle of exponential increase comes into play.

- A fourth measure or dimension occurs when God's people praise Him, for He says He "inhabits the praises of His people" (see Ps. 22:3). He is already in our midst but has chosen to manifest Himself upon us more powerfully in that atmosphere.

- A fifth measure is seen when the Temple of Solomon was dedicated: God came so profoundly that priests were incapacitated (see 1 Kings 8:10-11). No one could even stand, let alone play instruments or sing. They were completely undone at that measure of Presence.

I mention these five levels only as principles, in an effort to give a snapshot of how He longs to increase His manifestation upon His people. The day of Pentecost and the gift of the baptism in the Holy Spirit may in fact illustrate all of these principles combined as an entire city came under the influence of God's manifest Presence.

These various measures of Presence are recorded both in history and in Scripture. Reformation and revival history shows us what's available. The responsibility for the measure of God's Presence that we carry lies with us. We always have what we earnestly want.

Living for One Thing

It's easy to get so preoccupied with the vision for our lives that we miss the process entirely. We are here to grow into the maturity of Jesus, bring as many converts to Him as possible, and transform everywhere we have authority and influence. What we sometimes fail to realize is that all of those assignments are impossible. Every one of them. But strangely, they are possible if they are the fruit of something else. And this is *something* we can actually do. Let me explain.

We are called into fellowship with God. In this process, He has made it possible for us not only to come to know Him, but also to have Him live inside of us and even rest upon us. Everything we could ever want out of life flows from that one privilege. King David understood this concept better than most New Testament believers. He referred to it as the *one thing* (see Ps. 27:4). All of life gets reduced to one thing—how we steward the Presence of God. Stewarding the Presence of God, hosting the Presence, is the only way these impossible dreams can be accomplished.

The fulfillment of these dreams is actually the byproduct of hosting Him well. Jesus affirmed this principle for life when He taught, *"But seek first His kingdom and His righteousness, and all these things will be added to you"* (Matt. 6:33). The Kingdom of God is not something separate from His actual Presence. The Kingdom has a King. In reality, the Kingdom of God is within the Presence of the Spirit of God. *"For the kingdom of God is...in the Holy Spirit"* (Rom. 14:17). This command by Jesus is to prioritize our lives down to the *one thing* which is eventually evidenced by righteous living.

I once had the Lord wake me in the night with His voice. He said that He watches over the watch of those who watch the Lord. It's been a number of years since that encounter. Thinking of that moment still excites and yet puzzles me all at the same time. The "watch" represents God-given responsibilities. It's what a watchman does—he looks over his responsibility to make sure things are safe and properly taken care of. God was essentially telling me that He would watch over my watch (responsibilities) if I would make "watching Him" my only responsibility. It was His invitation for me to become Presence-centered.

When we discuss our responsibilities in life, many good things come to our minds. But for me now it always boils down to the one thing—His Presence. What do I do with His Presence? What place does the manifest Presence of God have with how I think and live? Does the Presence of God affect the vision and focus of my life? What is the impact of the *one thing* on my behavior?

The Gate to a Transformed City

In Acts chapter one, Jesus appeared to five hundred people, telling them not to leave Jerusalem until they received the promise of the Father. The remaining eleven disciples of Jesus were a part of this group. The eleven had already received the Holy Spirit in John 20, but were still commanded to stay in Jerusalem for what the Father had promised. A prayer meeting was formed. After ten days, only one hundred and twenty people were left.

As highly regarded as this day is in our hearts, I'm not sure we really see the significance. On the day of Pentecost, the baptism in the Holy Spirit was given. This baptism in the Holy Spirit is called the Father's Promise. The Father, the One who only gives good gifts, has given us this gift. All life flows only from Him. He is the One who is the orchestrator and conductor of life, and He has given a promise. And this is it. This is His special gift. It's a promise that reintroduces us to the original purpose for humanity—a people suited to carry the fullness of God on earth (see Eph. 3:19). This is only possible through the baptism in the Holy Spirit—a baptism of fire!

> *And suddenly **there came from heaven** a noise like a violent rushing wind, and it filled the whole house where they were sitting* (Acts 2:2).

A noise came from Heaven. Two worlds met. It was like a violent rushing wind. The word *rushing* is *phero*. Out of the 67 times that word is translated in the New Testament, it is *rushing* only once. The other times it has the meaning *to carry*, *to bear*, or *to bring forth*. It would be foolish for me to suggest changing how it's translated. But I would like to suggest adding the *bring forth* aspect to our understanding of its meaning. So then, could the word *rushing* imply that this was a noise, a violent wind, that *carried* or *brought forth* something from its place of origin to its destiny—from Heaven to earth? I think so.

Noise can be translated *roar*. God spoke the worlds into being. His word is the creative force. *"By the word of the Lord the heavens were made, and by the breath of His mouth all their host"* (Ps. 33:6; see Gen. 1:3-24). This sound could have come from the mouth of God releasing something on the earth that the prophets longed to see and be a part of from the beginning. Add to this the fact that God Himself rides on the wind (Ps. 104:3). We then see that this is a moment when God, riding on wind, a sound, Heaven's breath, is restoring humankind to purpose. Without question, the most dramatic invasion of Heaven to earth happened in this moment. It was *the* defining moment. This is what the Father promised.

The Airwaves Carry Heaven's Sound

This sound did in fact carry a reality from that world into this one. This heavenly sound transformed the atmosphere over the city of Jerusalem. In one moment it was changed from the city that crucified Jesus to a city that wanted to know what to do to be saved. How did that happen? Through sound—a sound from Heaven. Both sound and light are vibrations. And on this day it was the vibration of Heaven that introduced a different drumbeat to a city that was unaware of whose drumbeat they were marching to. For the first time they could see.

The house of God is the gate of Heaven. Remember, it's the house built on the edge of two worlds. And right here we see the effect on its surroundings when they became open to what God is doing. There was a literal release of something from that world, *through the gate* into this one. And a city was positioned to experience unfathomable change.

The heavenly sound was heard and experienced on earth. The roar of Heaven summoned this city to its purpose and call. In this moment, two worlds collided, and the inferior realm of darkness gave way to the superior nature of His Kingdom. We have the unique privilege of carrying His Presence. In doing so, we cause this kind of conflict so that these two realities, called Heaven and earth, could dance together in perfect harmony.

This picture is similar to the picture given at Jesus' baptism in that it was a violent activity from Heaven. It upset the powers that were accustomed to occupying that space. And in Acts 2, the Holy Spirit was released in the same way as at Jesus' baptism—this time upon His people instead of upon Jesus. It's important to note that violence in the spiritual realm is always a peace-filled moment for His people. That's how the Prince of Peace can crush satan under our feet (see Rom. 16:20). Another way to put it is every peace-filled moment you experience brings terror to the powers of darkness. Only in the Kingdom of God is peace a military tool.

A City Restored

When that mysterious sound was released at Pentecost, thousands of people began to gather to the one hundred and twenty at the upper room. It was nine o'clock in the morning. People were still preparing for the day. But they dropped everything. Men laid down their tools, women had their children put down their toys. A sound filled the air that also filled their hearts. Imagine an atmospheric shift over an entire city.

This is the city that rose up to crucify Jesus. His Presence among them was the one good thing they had, and they destroyed it by responding to the spirit of murder, the one thing civilized people pride themselves on resisting. Yet what erupted out of the heart of God, the sound that was released through that open Heaven, erupted over an entire city. No one knows why the crowd gathered in front of the upper room. No handbills or posters were distributed. No announcements were made. But a sound was released over them that cleared the air for the first time in their lives. Their thoughts were clear. They could reason. They sensed divine purpose. It seemed as though God was summoning people. And that's exactly what happened.

Growing up, I always thought people gathered because the one hundred and twenty were speaking in tongues, which was in the people's native languages. But that doesn't make sense, especially for an international city where foreign visitors are common. They gathered to a sound, an indistinguishable sound, one that reached deep into the hearts of people. Apart from an act of God, it would be nearly impossible to cause people to leave their businesses, homes, and activity centers to gather for no known reason. This sound called to something deep within the heart of this city, calling to restore it to its original purpose. This city was to be known as a city of His Presence. King David made that dedication so many years earlier in the tabernacle he built within that city which was dedicated to 24/7 worship.

To illustrate the nature of this sound, I like to compare it to that of a musical instrument. A gifted musician can get an almost magical sound out of the saxophone as they skillfully breathe across the reed properly placed in the mouthpiece of the instrument. Now in the same way, consider the breath of God blowing across the reed of the hearts of one hundred and twenty people releasing a sound over a city that changed its atmosphere. When you change an atmosphere, you change a destiny. That's what people heard. A *harmonic* sound that came because one hundred and twenty were together in *unity*, not only with each other, but with the Spirit of the resurrected Christ. That is the sound that was heard some 2,000 years ago. It was a sound that initiated the ushering in of 3,000 people in one day. A momentum was created through this open Heaven that made it so people were *added* to their numbers daily (see Acts 2:47). That continued until it opened even more and they moved from *addition* to *multiplication* (see Acts 9:31).

Once a Coward, Not Always a Coward

When Peter saw the crowds gather, he had an uncontrollable urge to preach. This man, who was a coward only days ago when questioned by a servant girl (see Mark 14:69), now stood heroically before thousands to proclaim the good news. Remember, it wasn't just the fact that he had to give witness to a large crowd. It was before a crowd that was now mocking what they saw once they were drawn to that place. This sermon came in the midst of the most unusual manifestations by God's chosen people. The crowd thought the hundred and twenty people were drunk. But often what we think drives the world away from the Gospel actually brings them to it. It only drives away those who have been taught against it. (Many think God's reputation is somehow protected when our dignity is preserved. And yet God is constantly asking us to lay down our rights—even to dignity.) Courage rose up in Peter's heart, and he made sense of it all and brought forth the perfect message for this moment. Cowards are only *one touch from God* away from becoming courageous preachers with great power.

"What must we do to be saved?" (See Acts 2:37.) That's quite a response from the people who crucified Jesus only weeks earlier. Was it Peter's sermon? While I don't want to take away from the moment of profound bravery, Peter preached under an open Heaven. This atmosphere carried the sound of Heaven that changed the mindsets of an entire city in moments. His message was quite brief. But it was filled with power, and it brought understanding so that the nervous mockery stopped and the real issues of the heart could be seen. In this one message, 3,000 people were saved. This becomes the devil's worst possible nightmare. Suddenly, things progressed from the anointing/open Heaven existing over one Man, Jesus, to the one hundred and twenty, and now imparted to 3,000 new believers. The potential of this movement is unlimited, until the whole earth is filled with His glory! And that is God's intention through those who host Him well, all while yielding to the wonderful Holy Spirit.

What It's All About

I have a Pentecostal background, for which I am very thankful. My forefathers paid quite a price to preach and defend that the baptism in the Spirit and speaking in tongues is still for today. I owe it to them to do nothing to take away from their accomplishments, but to add all I can. Having said that, I have seen that many have come to the wrong conclusions about this Holy Spirit baptism. It's not for tongues (which I believe is important and available to *everyone*). It's for *power.* And it's not just power for miracles. It's so that the power-charged atmosphere of Heaven can rest upon a person, which forces a shift in the atmosphere over a home, business, or city. This baptism is to make us living witnesses and examples of the resurrection of Jesus—the ultimate display of Heaven's power. The Spirit of the resurrected Christ is what filled the air on the day of Pentecost.

The Long Prayer Meeting

I can only imagine that after ten days of praying together they were tired and had probably exhausted everything they could think of to pray about. Suddenly, their affection for Jesus was taken to a level they had never known or experienced before. Their spirits became empowered by the Holy Spirit in that *suddenly* moment. They were alive, really alive for the first time in their lives. They spoke of things they didn't understand. Two worlds collided. And the understanding of God that exists in that heavenly realm actually influenced the language of the one hundred and twenty here on earth. They spoke of the mysterious ways and the mighty deeds of God.

This baptism is likened to *wine* and not *water*. Water refreshes while wine influences. When God calls a particular baptism a *baptism of fire*, it is obviously not one of mere refreshing. Heaven has come to influence earth in this baptism. But when that rushing mighty wind came and the language of Heaven poured forth from their lips, they also were refreshed by what influenced them. Paul would later point out that praying in tongues edifies us. There's little doubt about that happening to this small group. To top it off, they were speaking something so completely satisfying, so accurate and powerful, that it was like experiencing a completely new day. And they were. This heavenly language came as an eruption from their hearts. But for the first time in their lives, and actually in all of history, they said what needed to be said perfectly without missing it or falling short in one way or another.

The Spirit of God spoke through them with brilliant understanding of whom He was exalting. Their praise went right from the Spirit of God, through their yielded lips, to God Himself. In this instance, the human intellect was bypassed. They were *"speaking of the mighty deeds of God"* (Acts 2:11). This time, the language was a language of praise—not prayer. Imagine the privilege it was to speak of the great mysteries of God's nature over a city that had rejected Him. It was intoxicating, to say the least. The intention of the Lord is that this baptism of fire would ignite every heart. This would be best expressed by a people who were presence-driven instead of ministry-driven. It's not about what I can accomplish for God. It's all about who goes with me and my doing all I can to protect that most valuable connection.

When More Leads to More

A few years after this great outpouring of the Spirit, things were still going quite well. In fact, the numbers were increasing daily, and miracles would shake an entire city. Peter and John released a miracle to a lame man that seemed to shake up everyone (see Acts 3:1-10). They were credited as having great boldness. As a result, they were arrested, interrogated, persecuted, and finally released. Upon their release they went to a prayer meeting and prayed for more boldness.

> *And now, Lord, take note of their threats, and grant that Your bond-servants may speak Your word with all confidence, while You extend Your hand to heal, and signs and wonders take place through the name of Your holy servant Jesus* (Acts 4:29-30).

And the Spirit of God came in again. We always need more.

Many who speak in tongues think they are full of the Holy Spirit. Being full of Holy Spirit is not evidenced in tongues; it is evidenced by being full. How do you know when a glass is completely full? It runs over. Peter, on the day of Pentecost, is filled with Holy Spirit. In Acts 4, Peter joins many others in a prayer meeting. Their overwhelming expression was to cry out for more. Peter prayed for more. He did not pray for relief in the midst of persecution, but instead for more boldness, that expression that sometimes offends, so that he could go deeper into the realms of darkness and pull out more victims. And the Bible says:

> *And when they had prayed, the place where they had gathered together was shaken, and they were all filled with the Holy Spirit and began to speak the word of God with boldness* (Acts 4:31).

In Acts 2, Peter is filled. In Acts 4, he needs to be refilled. Why? If you are doing this right, you must get filled often. There is one baptism. But we are to live in such a way that we give away all we get, while our capacity for Him increases. When we live full of the Holy Spirit, experiencing overflow, only more of Him will do. Needing to be refilled is not a sign of something gone wrong. Continual dependence on *more* is a good thing.

Purpose of Outpouring

It is so easy to assume that something like the baptism in the Holy Spirit is primarily to make us more useful in ministry. That makes us *top heavy* in the sense that we become *professionals* in areas of life that were really reserved for *romantics*. My friend Bob Kilpatrick would call that approach *law* instead of *art*.[1] There are parts of our walk with Christ that should never be reduced to a list of goals and accomplishments. Instead, this unimaginable privilege of carrying His presence should never reduce me to a laborer for God. The decision of being a servant or a friend is still being chosen by people around us every day. While it is one of my highest privileges to serve Him completely, my labor is the byproduct of my love. This baptism introduces us to intimacy at the highest possible level.

The heart of God in this matter is clearly seen in this amazing prophecy from Ezekiel. *"I will not hide **my face** from them any longer, for I will have poured out **my Spirit**"* (Ezek. 39:29). In the outpouring of the Holy Spirit is the revelation of the face of God. There is nothing greater. *"In the light of the king's face is life, and his favor is like a cloud with the spring rain"* (Prov. 16:15). Rain is a biblical metaphor for the move of the Holy Spirit, thus the term *outpouring*. This verse also links God's face, His favor, with the outpouring of His Spirit.[2]

The revelation of the face of God through the outpouring of the Spirit is made available to everyone. The outpouring in Acts 2 was the beginning. The outpouring of the Spirit is the fulfillment of the quest for God's face. This means that wherever we go in revival, we can't go past the face. The only direction to go is to cry out for a greater measure of His Presence in the outpouring. Psalm 80 links the favor of His face with the work of His hand. The righteous who seek His face in intimacy are those who can be used to do great exploits. Heroes of the faith became men and women *of [God's] right hand* (Ps. 80:17). He put them on like a glove and used them to display His signs and wonders. We must be those who see what's available and contend for a greater measure of His favor to be upon us.

Moses experienced the transforming Presence on his own face. It was the result of his own face-to-face encounter with God. The outpouring brings us to His face again. And believe it or not, Moses' experience pales by comparison. *"How will the ministry of the Spirit fail to be even more with glory?"* (2 Cor. 3:8). So then, as we prioritize hosting His presence, we learn to release His face of favor into the earth. That is what people of great favor do.

ENDNOTES

1. *The Art of Being You: How to Live as God's Masterpiece* by Bob and Joel Kilpatrick tackles this issue beautifully. It is from Zondervan Publishing.

2. My book, *Face to Face with God*, from Strang Publishing takes this theme as its primary focus.

7

The Ultimate Prototype

Somewhere around 10 years after the day of Pentecost, the church was experiencing growing pains again. It happened at least once before in Acts 6 when some of the widows were not having their basic needs met. It became apparent that to take care of people correctly they needed people who could give themselves to practical service while the apostles were able to commit themselves to prayer and the study of Scriptures. The new team of servants was called *deacons*. But now there was a much bigger problem. Gentiles were getting saved in great numbers, and they were affecting the culture and nature of this new organism called the Church. Some might say that the tail was now wagging the dog.

It had taken quite awhile for the gentiles to become a real emphasis for the church of Jews. In fact, they were quite happy with life together in Jerusalem, that is, until persecution hit. (Even open heavens do not guarantee there will not be opposition. As long as there are people who make agreements with the devil, there will be varying levels of opposition to God's people.) The church then spread around the known world while the apostles stayed behind. Two things happened. One is that people who were not thought to be leaders found themselves in a place where leadership is required.

Sometimes we don't know what we have in us until it's required of us to serve. They stepped into a greater anointing and found out rather quickly what they had. People got saved in significant numbers. Then, they started to give attention to the commission given to them close to 10 years earlier from Jesus Himself. "Go into all the world…" (see Matt. 28:19). And then:

> *You will receive power when the Holy Spirit has come upon you; and you shall be My witnesses both in Jerusalem, and in all Judea and Samaria, and even to the remotest part of the earth* (Acts 1:8).

The movement outside of Jerusalem was growing so quickly that they called for help from their spiritual leaders, the apostles. And they brought the much-needed help, both in the miracle realm and in the governmental role. It seems that the shift in focus was almost by accident. This is when the church started having issues with the gentile believers.

Who Invaded My Pew?

I've seen this happen in our day. Church members get quite comfortable, and then revival hits. Those who reject it of course won't call it an actual move of God. But there's always a great influx of people who have "not paid the light bills" all these years who come into the church, excited, wondering why people just sit there. When you add to the mix a great number of converts, things really get exciting. New believers are known to bring all kinds of issues to the surface. My uncle used to say, "Every household needs a two year old." He was speaking naturally. But the same is true spiritually. Priorities get refined automatically when children are around. Chuck Smith of Calvary Chapel in Costa Mesa made such a choice when confronted this problem at the beginning of the Jesus People Movement. The members were concerned about their new carpet being soiled by the barefoot hippies. Pastor Chuck told them that he would tear out the carpet then. Priorities. Simple but profound.

Of course, when you have a need to justify criticism you have to find a spiritual term to make it OK. Holiness or discernment is often used for such moments. It amazes me how many people, who have prayed for revival for years, will leave a church once they get it. Great moves of God upset everything. Nothing is left untouched. As fishers of men our job is to catch them and let Him clean them.

The apostles had many concerns. Most of it dealt with issues of holiness, which is a very legitimate issue. They had to settle on what salvation by grace really looked like. These new believers were challenging things that might have never been questioned by the Jewish believers. When you add to the mix the fact that there were those with unhealthy attachments to the old way of doing things, as in Mosaic Law, there was a real uncertainty about it all. I'm sure each apostle had their convictions as to how things should be.

There's no doubt of their commitment to salvation by God's grace. But there is also strong evidence that they didn't think alike, but more importantly they didn't want to present multiple standards as they continued to successfully evangelize the known world. They had some decisions to make.

The First of Its Kind

The first leaders' conference was called for this elite group of apostles. They convened in Jerusalem, the God-chosen head-quarters for the Church. As they met they presented the issues. But the way they came to a conclusion is quite fascinating. They shared testimonies. They each had stories to tell pertaining to God's outpouring among the Gentiles. As they heard the stories they began to recognize a theme: God poured out His Spirit upon Gentiles before they knew enough to get themselves acquainted with Jewish traditions. In fact, He seemed to move among them with little regard for their own readiness for an authentic Holy Spirit outpouring.

What moves me in this part of the story is that they actually developed their theology around what they saw God do. They didn't approach the issue with an exegetical study of Jesus' sermons to find out what to do. That kind of study is noble and good. But you usually need the move of God to be happening before you get insight about what it is that is happening. I've never heard of anyone studying their way into a revival.

Now I realize that this seems to be treading in dangerous territory for so many, but to me the risk is worth it. Why do you think new moves of God almost always start with people who don't know what they're doing? At least in part, we limit God to our present understanding of how God moves, all while praying that God would do a new thing among us. What we know can keep us from what we need to know if we don't remain a novice. When we become experts we have chosen where we level off in our maturity. He still requires that primary advancements in the Kingdom be made through childlikeness.

Can I Get a Witness!

James, the apostle at Jerusalem, brought the testimony time to a biblical conclusion. He said, *"With this the words of the prophets agree!"* (Acts 15:15). What he shared in the following moments was possibly new to him, as there's no record of this revelation being commonplace before this moment. It appears to me that God actually dropped this Scripture into his heart as they were talking. In other words, God gave Scripture to James to back up the legitimacy of the stories being told. Biblical backing is vital. But I doubt there has ever been a great move of God where everything that happened was preceded by revelation—they understood it before it happened. Experience gives understanding. *Complete understanding first* seems to violate the issue of trust that is deeply valued in the heart of God for His people. At any rate, James got a word from God to give the needed biblical backing.

Here is the account:

*After they had stopped speaking, James answered, saying, "Brethren, listen to me. Simeon has related how **God first concerned Himself about taking** from among the Gentiles **a people for His name**. With this the words of the Prophets agree, just as it is written, 'After these things I will return, and I will rebuild the **Tabernacle of David** which has fallen, and I will rebuild its ruins, and **I will restore it**, so **that the rest of mankind may seek the Lord**, and all the gentiles who are called by My name,' says the Lord, who makes these things known from long ago. Therefore it is my judgment that we do not trouble those who are turning to God from among the Gentiles, but that we write to them that they abstain from things contaminated by idols and from fornication and from what is strangled and from blood* (Acts 15:13-20).

Remember, the problem had everything in the world to do with Gentiles. The apostles knew they could be saved, but they were unsure of how much of their Jewish religion and history was important for these new believers.

Notice, in the Acts 15 passage is the mention of the Tabernacle of David. This is the one story in the Old Testament that provides greater basis for this theme of the Christian life than any other (see 2 Sam. 6; 1 Chron. 15). It is a story of heart, presence, extravagant worship, and of unusual purpose among the nations. Even grace itself takes center stage in this story.

David's Tabernacle became the backdrop for life as we know it today in the New Testament church. It had to do with King David, who functioned as a priest, and is even called a prophet in Acts 2. To me David is the greatest example of life under grace in the Old Testament. King, priest, and prophet—a complete prophetic picture of the Christ to come. It also portrayed the coming New Testament believer.

David's Tabernacle existed for close to 40 years. It was a completely new approach to God—the priests worshiped God for 24 hours a day, 7 days a week, without a blood sacrifice.

God's House, Old Testament Style

There were several houses of God in the Old Testament.

The first was in the Genesis 28 story of Jacob meeting with God on the side of the mountain. It was called *Bethel*, which means the house of God. It is covered in chapter one of this book. There was actually no building. God was there. That's what made it His house.

The *Tabernacle of Moses* gave us a picture of Jesus. Every piece of furniture spoke of something about the coming Messiah.

It was built according the specific details that God gave Moses on the mountain in a face-to-face meeting.

The *Temple of Solomon* was more glorious and beautiful than anything ever built on earth. It was humanity's best effort to give God something to dwell in that was consistent with His worth. It was built according very precise plans, representing the permanent dwelling of God.

The *restored temple of Solomon* was built to twice the size of the original. When God restores He restores to a place greater than before restoration was needed. It did not contain the beauty of the previous temple. Those who saw the former glory wept at the sight of the restored house. Those who didn't see the former house rejoiced at this one.

The *Tabernacle of David* was built for worship. No description of building materials was ever mentioned and no size is ever given. The Ark of the Covenant was there. The presence of God rested upon the ark. Priests worshiped 24 hours a day—different shifts were taken so this could be accomplished continually. The two outstanding factors are God was there in His glory and priests ministered to God nonstop.[1]

Who Are We?

The prophet Amos prophesied of a time when David's tabernacle would be rebuilt.

> *"In that day I will raise up the fallen booth of David, and wall up its breaches; I will also raise up its ruins and rebuild it as in the days of old; that they may possess the remnant of Edom and all the nations who are called by My name,"* declares the Lord who does this (Amos 9:11-12).

He identifies the rebuilding of David's tabernacle as that which releases the fruit He wants—*possessing the remnant of Edom and all the nations called by His name.* The restoration project would release a specific fruit—Gentiles would come into the Kingdom.

James identifies the tree by its fruit. In other words, he noticed that Gentiles were brought in like the prophets said (the fruit), which enabled him to identify the work that God was doing on the earth. The work of God was the restoration of the Tabernacle of David, which is the tree in this metaphor. It is that specific work of God that produced the fruit. More specifically, the church is the house that houses a priesthood—a worshiping community that offers spiritual sacrifices to God.

> *You also, as living stones, are being built up as a spiritual house for a holy priesthood, to offer up spiritual sacrifices acceptable to God through Jesus Christ* (1 Peter 2:5).

That priesthood of worshipers is God's restoration project. The worshiping church brought about an open heaven whereby Gentiles would see and understand truth for the first time. Worship cleared the airwaves, just as it happened in Jerusalem in Acts 2.

I love how James translates verse 12. Amos said, *"That they may possess the remnant of Edom and all the nations who are called by My name"* (Amos 9:12). But James said, quoting the Amos passage, *"That the rest of mankind may seek the Lord, and all the gentiles who are called by My name"* (Acts 15:17). He interprets it into a New Testament context. (Jesus did the same thing with Psalms 8:2. He took *ordained strength* and turned it into *perfected praise* in Matthew 21:16 NKJV.) Edom, in the original statement by Amos, is the land of Esau. Esau sold his birthright. He became the biblical example of the rest of humankind, who had no natural right to an inheritance. Yet because of grace, we are grafted into the plan of God for His people.

The bottom line in this prophecy is that you'll know when God is restoring David's Tabernacle as it will be signified by Gentiles coming to faith in Jesus.

Building What?

So what is being rebuilt? The church, with its unique Davidic anointing for the Presence, is the fulfillment of this prophecy from Amos. We are the community of worshipers whose primary focus is ministering to God Himself. But the significance for this book lies in this one fact—only priests could carry God's Presence. God is pretty insistent upon that requirement.

To see what God is rebuilding and how it affects us in this unique priority we must first learn about the original project. David's passion paves the way.

Good Intentions Can Kill

Saul was the king before David. As king Saul had little regard for the Presence of God (Ark of the Covenant), David became king of Judah and then Israel. He was acquainted with the Presence of God from his time on the backside of the desert, caring for his father's sheep. He was a worshiper. He no doubt learned of God's desire for yielded hearts instead of the blood of bulls and goats in his private times with God. Some of God's best lessons can't be learned in a class, they can only be learned on a journey.

David immediately made arrangements to bring the Ark into Jerusalem and place it in the tent that he pitched for that purpose (see 2 Sam. 6:17). It was David's number-one priority. There was nothing even close to the priority of God's Presence being with David, being with Israel. The story is exciting, intriguing, and deadly.

The nation of Israel planned for this day. They lined the streets to witness the ceremony of worship orchestrated to bring the presence of God into the city of David, Jerusalem. Those who could play instruments brought them in a sacrificial celebration to honor God as He came. The finest ox cart was obtained for the event. Priests took their places as they ushered in the Holy One. But one of the oxen stumbled and nearly upset the cart that carried the Ark. Uzzah reached out his hand to steady the Ark out of his concern for the Presence. The anger of the Lord burned against him for his irreverence. God killed him. His Presence cannot be manhandled. This story alone should sober the hearts and minds of those who would tend to use the anointing for personal gain. He will not be commandeered by man.

David left the Ark in the house of Obed-Edom. All in his household prospered because of the Presence (see 2 Sam. 6:11).

When in Doubt, Read the Instructions

To say David was scared is a great understatement. He was so sure this was the thing to do. His hunger for God was sincere and legitimate. But sincerity alone will not save anyone. Drinking strychnine thinking it's a fruit juice doesn't make it any less poisonous.

When David heard that the household of Obed-Edom was prospering in all ways, he became more diligent to find out what went wrong the day Uzzah died. He apparently turned to the Scriptures for insight. (It's not wrong to be motivated by blessing. Even Jesus endured the Cross because of the joy before Him (see Heb. 12:2). Reward is a huge part of the Kingdom consciousness.) David found out that only priests could carry the Presence (see 1 Chron. 15:2). Forever. I love whenever I find a command or promise that has the word *forever* in it. It automatically means there's a principle involved that will carry over into this lifestyle of grace as well as our heavenly existence. Such is the case with this verse. Only priests can carry His presence. Period.

God will not ride on ox carts, even though the Philistines seemed to get away with it (see 1 Sam. 4-6). The presence of God will not rest on anything we make. He rests on us. I believe that applies to organizations, buildings, etc. People will often look at institutions that have been created to facilitate great ministries.

But no matter how great the organization, the by-laws, or the reputation, God doesn't rest upon those things. It's people. Yielded people have the privilege of carrying (hosting) God into life's situations.

Do-Overs

David announced the new plan to usher God's presence into his city. The people were ready. The priests were ready. The priestly musicians trained for the day. Those assigned to carry the ark of His Presence probably wondered about the fearfully exciting privilege involved in their job. After all, the last guy to get that close to the Ark died. But this time they had the will of God revealed in Scripture to support the process.

This story is one of the greatest stories in the Bible. It should be known forward and backward by every believer, as it is key to clearly fulfill our role in this day.[2] It is our story, ahead of time.

The day came. King David stripped himself of his kingly garments and put on a priest's tunic, basically a priest's undergarment. This was not something a king would be seen in normally. But then David was not a normal king. He would become known as the man after God's heart—the man of God's Presence. After six steps, they stopped and sacrificed an ox to the Lord. He then danced before the Ark with all of his might.

This must have been a fearfully beautiful sight. All of Israel was lining the streets, rejoicing in the actual Presence of God. The musicians played with great skillfulness. As much as it was possible, a nation showed up for an event. The grandeur, the magnificence and sheer volume must have been overwhelming. Everyone present was impacted by this *once in a lifetime* experience.

It is worth noting that the Ark of the Covenant (the Presence of God) followed David into Jerusalem. Wherever David danced, God followed. He responds to our offerings. In this story, it's an offering of thanksgiving and praise expressed in the dance. Many respond to God once His Presence is realized. But some respond before He actually comes. They are the ones who usher in the Presence of the King of Glory. Another way of looking at it is God showed up wherever King David danced in an undignified fashion. It might surprise us to find out what is attractive to Him.

Someone's Missing

There was one notable absentee. Michal, the daughter of Saul, looked at the event through the palace window. Extreme worship always looks to be extreme foolishness to those who stand at a distance. Some things can only be understood from within. Such is the case with authentic worship.

Michal was appalled at David's lack of regard for how people perceived his passion, his humility in attire, and his complete lack of public decorum. Instead of greeting him with honor, she tried to shame him.

But when David returned to bless his household, Michal the daughter of Saul came out to meet David and said, "How the king of Israel distinguished himself today! He uncovered himself today in the eyes of his servants' maids as one of the foolish ones shamelessly uncovers himself!" (2 Samuel 6:20)

His response was very bold in many ways.

So David said to Michal, "It was before the Lord, who chose me above your father and above all his house, to appoint me ruler over the people of the Lord, over Israel; therefore I will celebrate before the Lord. I will be more lightly esteemed than this and will be humble in my own eyes, but with the maids of whom you have spoken, with them I will be distinguished" (2 Samuel 6:21-22).

David made it clear that God chose him above her father. This was a biting comment to say the least. Her disregard for the Presence of God revealed that she carried some of the same *lack of value* for the Presence that her father Saul had lived by during his reign. Dumbing down our emphasis on the Presence should never be to accommodate the Michals in the house. He followed that comment stating that she basically hadn't seen anything yet. In other words, if that embarrassed her, her future was not too bright. David was just getting warmed up. Tragically, *"Michal the daughter of Saul had no child to the day of her death"* (2 Sam. 6:23).

Whenever someone despises extravagant worship, they put themselves in an extremely dangerous position. Barrenness is the natural result of despising worship. In doing so they are rejecting the reason why we're alive. Barrenness and the absence of worship go hand in hand. This scene happened again during Jesus' ministry. It was when the costly ointment was poured over Jesus. All the disciples were upset (see Matt. 26:8). The devil actually doesn't mind worship that is tame. Extreme worship exposes religion[3] in everyone.

There is a wonderful verse that speaks to the effect of extreme worship on barrenness itself.

> *"Shout for joy, O barren one, you who have borne no child; break forth into joyful shouting and cry aloud, you who have not travailed; for the sons of the desolate one will be more numerous than the sons of the married woman,"* says the Lord (Isaiah 54:1).

What a promise. In this chapter we find a barren woman who is exhorted to shout for joy *before* she becomes pregnant. The end result is that she will have more children than the one who has been having children all along. This provides quite the prophetic picture. The people who are people of worship, regardless of circumstances, will become fruitful in ways beyond reason.

Anyone can get happy after the miracle has come. Show me someone who celebrates before the answer, and I'll show you someone who is about to experience the answer. This is the nature of faith—it looks ahead and lives accordingly.

Restored to Purpose

Perhaps it would be appropriate to reintroduce the Genesis 1:28 passage in this context, as worshipers truly will *"be fruitful and multiply, and fill the earth, and subdue it."* Is this example of Michal and the Isaiah 54 woman really that significant? I believe it is. In David's Tabernacle we are connected to our original purpose as worshipers to be carriers of the glory and restore fruitfulness to the barren places in the lives of those who have suffered at the enemy's hands. The devil came to *"steal and kill and destroy"* (John 10:10). Jesus came to defeat the devil, expose his works, and reverse their effects. He came to give life. We have inherited that privileged assignment of enforcing the victory of Christ in those same ways. Worshipers just do that by nature.

The New Was in the Old

Sometimes we read Old Testament stories and accept them without realizing how dramatic or revolutionary they actually are. Such is the case with David and his tabernacle.

Blood: The Law was in effect until Jesus lived a sinless life, suffered, and died in our place, paying the demand or price that the Law required because of sin.

Under the Old Covenant, the priest could only enter into God's Presence through a blood sacrifice. And then only the high priest could come into the Holy of Holies one day a year, the Day of Atonement. The Holy of Holies is the inner room where manifest Presence of God was—the only light was the glorious Presence of God. This is where the Ark of the Covenant was kept.

When David became king he sensed that God was looking for something else—priests who offer the sacrifices of thanksgiving and praise through the yielded and broken heart. This was done even though the Law he lived under forbade it. It was offered with musical instruments as well as the voices of the singers. In this context, every priest could come daily before God without having to bring a blood offering. This order of worship was done twenty-four hours a day, seven days a week. This of course spoke of the day when every believer, a priest according to First Peter 2:9, would come to God in boldness because of what Jesus accomplished on our behalf. This is what was referred to when James said David's booth was being rebuilt.

David was the man after God's heart. He had a perception of God that would not be fully realized until Jesus would come and shed His blood for all. David's experience was a prophetic foretaste of something to come. I believe it was David's hunger for God that enabled him to pull this experience into his day, even though it was reserved for another day.

This tent or tabernacle that David built for the Ark was placed on Mount Zion. I live in northern California. When we speak of a mountain, we are speaking of a significant piece of our geography. Mount Shasta is over 14,000 feet in elevation. Mount Zion, on the other hand, is a simple rise in the earth and is contained within the city of Jerusalem. Zion means "sunny place," as it is where the sun shines first. What it lacked in elevation, it more than made up for in significance. Significance is always more important than visibility.

Some of the statements about Mount Zion are quite amazing to consider.

- *"Beautiful in elevation, the joy of the whole earth, is Mount Zion in the far north, the city of the great King"* (Ps. 48:2). Mount Zion is to be the joy of the whole earth.

- *"Out of Zion, the perfection of beauty, God has shone forth"* (Ps. 50:2). Zion is perfect beauty. It is from there God shines forth.

- *"The Lord loves the gates of Zion more than all the other dwelling places of Jacob"* (Ps. 87:2). Gates are praise (see Isa. 60:19). He inhabits praise. And the praise/gates of Zion are His favorite dwelling places.

- *"Why do you look with envy, O mountains with many peaks, at the mountain which God has desired for His abode? Surely the Lord will dwell there forever"* (Ps. 68:16). All the other mountains are envious of Mount Zion. It is where God has chosen to dwell. And because it says "forever" it carries a New Testament application. It is referring to the worshiping community as His Mount Zion. Again, what it lacks in elevation it more than makes up for in significance.

Worship Affects Nations

Psalms is the great book of worship. Songs were written to exalt God. But something unique happened in a few of these psalms. The writer would start to make declarations about the nations rising up to give God glory. Decrees were made about every nation worshiping the one true God. Now, regardless of where you think this fits into God's plan for the nations, worshipers first declare it. Why? Worshipers are in a place to call nations into their purpose, into their God-given destiny. It is the sacred privilege of those who worship. Below are a few verses that lend themselves to that thought.

> *All the ends of the earth will remember and turn to the Lord, and all the families of the nations will worship before You* (Psalms 22:27).

> *Let the nations be glad and sing for joy; for You will judge the peoples with uprightness and guide the nations on the earth* (Psalms 67:4).

> *May His name endure forever; may His name increase as long as the sun shines; and let men bless themselves by Him; let all nations call Him blessed* (Psalms 72:17).

> *All nations whom You have made shall come and worship before You, O Lord, and they shall glorify Your name* (Psalms 86:9).

> *Praise the Lord, all nations; laud Him, all peoples!* (Psalms 117:1)

A Last-Days Surprise

There's a prophecy declared both by Isaiah and Micah that has spoken to my heart now for many years. It speaks of the mountain of God's house. This can be none other than Mount Zion. This is prophetically fulfilled in the last days. I believe that it is referring to the rebuilding of the Tabernacle of David—the New Testament combining of believers from all nations into one company of people called worshipers.

> *Now it will come about that in the last days the mountain of the house of the Lord will be established as the chief of the mountains, and will be raised above the hills; and all the nations will stream to it* (Isaiah 2:2; Micah 4:1).

Look at the effect of this house being established as chief of all mountains. *Chief* means *head*. This government will be the head of all governments. As a result all nations will stream to it, asking for the word of the Lord. I believe this is referring to the massive harvest that will take place before the end comes. It is brought about by worshipers. It is the rebuilding of the Tabernacle of David. Worship affects the destiny of nations.

ENDNOTES

1. The greatest present-day model of this that I know of is Mike Bickle's IHOP—The International House of Prayer, headquartered in Kansas City. It is a remarkable ministry, where worship and intercession have continued nonstop now for over ten years.

2. The finest materials I am aware of on this subject are from Ray Hughes at http://selahministries.com. I highly recommend both Ray and his materials.

3. Historically, religion is used as a good term. Of late it has largely been used to describe Christianity when it is in form without power, or ritual without life. It is in that sense that I use it.

8

Red-Letter Revival

Jesus Christ is perfect theology. What you think you know about God that cannot be found in the person of Jesus, you have reason to question. He is the standard—the only standard given for us to follow.

As simple as that thought is, I never cease to be amazed at how many people try to improve on the example Jesus gave us and create a new standard—one that is more relevant. There seem to be two extremes in this regard. One is the Old Testament prophet-type ministry, whose view of God and man are accurate for their time, but very incomplete in regards to this hour that we live in. It is missing one significant ingredient—Jesus, the reconciler. He fulfilled the demands of the Law and made reconciliation with God possible. He would not allow James and John to minister under that anointing when they asked for permission (Luke 9:54). That season is over! (See Luke 16:16.) And then there are the ones who take great efforts not to offend anyone with the gospel. Honestly, that did not seem to be a value that Jesus carried. The heart is good in the sense they want everyone included in the family. But if we water down Jesus' message and get converts, whose converts are they? If they did not hear the same gospel of abandonment of all to Jesus, then whose message did they hear? Do we honestly think that the people who were unwilling to sell all in Jesus' day would be any more converted in ours?

There has been a struggle in the church for millennia about two contrasting challenges: maintaining the standards that Jesus set without going backward. So many want the Old Time Religion so much that they try to preserve a day that no longer exists in the heart of God. The other is the challenge to stay relevant with the current culture. The challenge is difficult as many forsake the moorings of the simple gospel to become contemporary. Jesus is always contemporary, current, and relevant, more so than anything going on anywhere around us. The Father, Son, and Holy Spirit are ageless. They are relevance at its best.

Bible schools and seminaries prioritize teaching instead of doing. Greek and Hebrew are important, but not more important than learning to recognize His voice and release the miracle of healing to someone. Leadership courses are important, but not more important than being able to lead someone to Christ or through deliverance. Management of finances is a big emphasis, and should be, considering how many failures there are. But Jesus taught the importance of managing our tongues and our families as well as our money. These are only hard classes to teach when the professors have no experience. Therein lies the problem. People with theories are raising up a generation who are satisfied with theories. Many stop short of a divine encounter because they are satisfied with good theology. One is to lead us to the other.

Massive efforts are made to do church in a timely fashion so we can continue with the rest of our lives. Apparently, many have not yet discovered that we really don't have a life outside of Christ.

We can attend one of the many fine Bible schools and seminaries across our land and take many courses on the study of Scripture, on leadership, music, administration, how to debate with other religions, etc. These courses have their place. And I'm only choosing from the schools that are true Bible believing, born again preaching schools. Examine the courses. How many teach how to heal the sick or raise the dead? How many have classes on prayer and fasting, or casting out demons, or interceding for the nations until there's a change? The courses taught are good and valuable. But can they be more important than what Jesus commanded us to learn and do? Perhaps the reason they are not taught is that those who do the teaching don't know how. These things cannot be taught merely from the head. They are not concepts. Truth that is separate from experience is divisive by nature. Truth experienced is inclusive.

This doesn't even take into consideration the multitude of schools that now question everything from the virgin birth to the miracles of Christ. Those are an abomination. One of the most foolish thoughts to ever enter the mind of a person is the thought that the "God who is now" is not relevant. The church may lose its relevancy, but God never will.

We are never relevant because we mirror the culture of the world around us. We are relevant when we have become what the world longs for. So many are accustomed to the idea that the gospel is to be constantly rejected and only a few of us will make it. I believe that is in error. Jesus is the desire of the nations. When we as His people represent Him well, people find what they are looking for, as we illustrate the desires of their hearts. We are His body on earth, the only Jesus that many will see. The representation of Him must be accurate.

Red Letters

I heard a great message recently from a dear friend, Lou Engle. He leads one of the most important prayer movements in all of history. He preached a masterful message from the Sermon on the Mount, Matthew 5–7. Lou asserted that the words of Jesus, the life of Jesus, the ministry of Jesus, the example of Jesus, and the commission of Jesus are what our lives are to be patterned after. There is no Plan B in the Kingdom of God. God is quite confident in His ability to accomplish Plan A just fine.

Of all the things that Jesus taught that challenge me to my inner core, I am even more stunned by the things unsaid. He carried the person of the Holy Spirit into the earth. He illustrated a lifestyle that is within reach but must be reached for. It will not come to us. Much of what we need in life will be brought to us, but most of what we want we will have to go get. It's just the way of the Kingdom.

My beginning years in ministry were filled with teaching from the Old Testament. I don't mean I taught Mosaic Law. I just loved the stories and learned to make New Testament applications. Those were important years—years I would not trade. But something has happened to me in recent years that I also would not trade. Jesus has come alive to me in ways I never understood before. His example is the inspiration for this book. Looking at how He lived has provoked me to jealousy—He successfully carried the "Dove that remained."

Personal Jealousy

Since I've discovered Jesus lived His life in a way that we could follow, I have found myself jealous for many things that were so natural to Him. My heart burns, as though with lust, for something that Jesus carried that is available for all. It's free, but not cheap. Don't be offended by my use of the term "lust" in this context. It is the actual thought Paul used when teaching us to earnestly pursue spiritual gifts. It is obviously not sexual, but does involve an inner burning. This phrase means to lustfully pursue. It is way beyond the casual mental agreement to a concept. It is a wind-driven fire within us.

Picture this well-known story in Jesus' life: The streets are crowded with people who are hungry for more. Some are in pursuit of God; others just want to be close to this man who has become so famous for wonderful things. He has raised the dead, healed the sick, and has become the single subject of a whole town. People followed Jesus anywhere and everywhere. As this throng of people are walking down the road, a woman, a very desperate woman, sees her chance for a miracle. She has carried her affliction for many years without any hope of recovery. She presses into the crowd until Jesus is within reach. But she is way too embarrassed to talk to Him or even get His attention. She merely reaches out to touch the edge of His clothing.

Now a woman, having a flow of blood for twelve years, who had spent all her livelihood on physicians and could not be healed by any, came from behind and touched the border of His garment. And immediately her flow of blood stopped. And Jesus said, "Who touched Me?" When all denied it, Peter and those with him said, "Master, the multitudes throng and press You, and You say, 'Who touched Me?'" But Jesus said, "Somebody touched Me, for I perceived power going out from Me." Now when the woman saw that she was not hidden, she came trembling; and falling down before Him, she declared to Him in the presence of all the people the reason she had touched Him and how she was healed immediately. And He said to her, *"Daughter, be of good cheer; your faith has made you well. Go in peace"* (Luke 8:43-48).

It's important to understand that power in the Kingdom of God is in the form of a person. It is not a separate entity apart from God Himself. Jesus realized that anointing, the person of the

Holy Spirit was released from Him, by the demand of somebody else's faith. This really is amazing.

Now it's one thing to become aware of the Presence of God in worship, and quite another to realize when the Holy Spirit is released from us in ministry. On occasion, I have felt the anointing of the Holy Spirit released from my hands when I've prayed for someone for healing. It's so encouraging. But it is a whole new level to be so aware of the Holy Spirit who rests upon us that we notice when someone else's faith has put a demand on what we carry. It can be said that she made a withdrawal from Jesus' account. How aware of the person of the Holy Spirit do we have to be to notice such a release of power when it flows from us? Add to this equation that Jesus was walking and talking with others when this happened. To me, this is astonishing. He is conscious of the Presence even when He is talking to others or listening to their comments and questions. It is for this that I am most jealous.

A withdrawal was made from the One who has been given the Spirit without measure. An anointing cannot be depleted. It wasn't the lack of anointing He discovered. It was the Holy Spirit moving that He recognized—the Holy Spirit was released from Him. This amazes me beyond words.

A Dove on the Shoulders

One of my favorite stories in the Bible is of Jesus' water baptism. We've already looked at it in part. But there's one more part of the story that is central to this book. It is recorded in John's Gospel.

John testified saying:

I have seen the Spirit descending as a dove out of heaven, and He remained upon Him. I did not recognize Him, but He who sent me to baptize in water said to me, "He upon whom you see the Spirit descending and remaining upon Him, this is the One who baptizes in the Holy Spirit." I myself have seen, and have testified that this is the Son of God (John 3:32-34).

Jesus sets the stage for a whole new season. The Old Testament prophets modeled this possibility amazingly, especially for their day. They showed the impact of the Presence of God upon a person for a specific task. But it was Jesus who revealed this as a lifestyle. The Holy Spirit remained upon Him.

Now I realize that we are not to live by feelings. Emotions are wonderful, but not reliable indicators of God's Presence and moving. But there is a feeling that goes beyond emotions, and quite frankly can work regardless of our emotional state. It is the mood of the Holy Spirit Himself that we can become so in tune with that we move as He moves.

We know that the Holy Spirit lives in us as born-again believers. The amazing promise that accompanies this reality is that He will never leave us. What a promise. What a comfort this is. But the sad reality is that the Holy Spirit doesn't rest upon every believer. He is in me for my sake, but He is upon me for yours. When the Holy Spirit rests upon a person without withdrawing, it is because He has been made welcome in a most honorable way.

I often ask people what they would do if an actual dove landed on their shoulders. How would they walk around a room, or even go about their day if they didn't want the dove to fly away. The most common answer is carefully. It's a good answer. But it's not enough. It is this—every step must be with the dove in mind. This is what I believe to be the key to the Spirit that remains. He is the single greatest reference point, not only for direction and power in ministry, but actually for life itself. We've been chosen to carry the Presence of God. Amazing.

Stewarding the Relationship

I remember as a young man hearing someone talk about being full of the Spirit. Having strong Pentecostal roots, I didn't consider this a new subject. But what I heard taught that day was new. The man of God simply spoke of two verses, neither of which referred to the baptism in the Spirit. It's not as much in my heart to make a doctrinal statement right now as it is to make a relational statement. These two verses are guidelines.

Do not grieve the Holy Spirit of God (Ephesians 4:30).

Do not quench the Spirit (1 Thessalonians 5:19).

This simple insight took my focus from the expressions of the Spirit (gifts, etc.) and shifted them to what the Holy Spirit actually felt because of me. And the more I walk with the Holy Spirit, the more my priorities shift to contribute to this relationship. This opens up new realms in walking with God that I had not considered.

To not grieve the Holy Spirit is a command focused on the issue of sin: in thought, attitude, or action. "Grieve" is a word that means to cause sorrow or distress. It describes the pain the heart of the Holy Spirit can feel because of something we would do or allow in our lives. It is character centered. This is a boundary that must have the attention of anyone who is interested in hosting His Presence more powerfully.

To not quench the Holy Spirit is a command that zeroes in on the co-laboring aspect of our relationship. The word "quench" means to stop the flow of. The original language defines it as to extinguish, or put out. This word brilliantly uses two metaphors to illustrate this connection with God. "To stop the flow" could be illustrated by bending a garden hose in half until water no longer flows from it, while "extinguish" portrays the passion part of our walk with God. To lose passion for God always affects our ability to allow the Holy Spirit to flow from us to change circumstances around us. This verse is power centered.

A Failed Experiment?

I don't understand those who consider sin to be a light-hearted matter. It is especially disturbing when those individuals seem to be gifted in power ministry. This reality causes some to reject the gifts of the Spirit altogether. For them, it seems to be evidence enough that the gifts can't be from God because God would never use people walking in sin. Others go to the other extreme and are offended at God for allowing people who live in sin to still function in some measure of anointing. I agree; it is a great mystery. But perhaps we would be less troubled if we could realize that God always honors His Word, regardless of the vessel in question. His Word reveals His character, not ours. And to not respond to His Word is to violate the covenant He created.

Having said this, I sure hope we will soon come to a day when this nonsense of tolerating sin stops for us. To make up for this weakness in the body, many have taught that character is more important than power. I taught this myself for many years. We have devastating stories to prove our point. Our stories are missing one minor detail: Jesus didn't teach or practice it that way. In fact, when Jesus gave power and authority to His disciples in Luke 9, it was immediately followed by some of their biggest blunders. Right after the disciples received this impartation, they are found rejecting other followers of Jesus—exclusivity had poisoned their hearts. Previous to this, they spent considerable time arguing who was better than the other. They had just returned from ministry to their hometowns. It stands to reason that their success in power ministry had given each of them all the evidence needed to prove their points—they were the greatest! James and John topped it off by wanting to kill an entire city of Samaritans by calling down fire on them. The spirit of murder was unrecognized by them, all in the name of ministry and discernment. All of these huge blemishes came to light after the glorious moment when Jesus entrusted them with power and authority. Their character was seriously flawed. The greatest part of this mystery is that He followed what we might call a failed experiment in chapter 9 by releasing the same anointing over 70 others in Luke chapter 10. He entrusted power to people who were far from qualified to walk in extraordinary anointing. Sometimes true character can only be formed in the trenches of warfare and life.

Two Are Better Than One

It is true that power is not more important than character. But it is equally true that character is not more important than power. Whenever we make that mistake, the gifts of the Spirit become rewards and are no longer gifts. This emphasis has actually damaged our effectiveness in the gifts of the Spirit. In fact, this approach has caused as much damage in the area of supernatural gifting as flawed character has damaged our witness to the world. Both are essential. Character and power are the two legs we stand on, equal in importance.

For every gifted person without character, I can show you many people with character who have little power. That has been the focus of the church in my generation in most parts of the world. A lifestyle without power has been considered normal. As a result, they are making little difference in the world around them. We must stop grading on the curve, where our approval comes from fitting in to the accepted standard. We must return to Jesus Christ—perfect theology, the ultimate example of the gifts of the Spirit working in the context of the fruits of the Spirit: character and power.

It is interesting to note that the groups of people who walk in little power are much more inclined to believe that the church is going to get weaker and weaker before the end of time comes.

They are prone to a view of the last days where very few will actually endure to the end. This perspective seems to legitimize their powerlessness, giving it a purpose. It's ridiculous.

On the other hand, those who walk in power see the desperate condition of the world, but also see the world's openness to God when the impossibilities of their lives yield to the name of Jesus through our lips. When the church discovers who she is, she no longer wants to be rescued. There's a big difference between rescued from the big bad devil and being taken up for a wedding. And only one is acceptable for a believing believer.

We are able to maintain our focus by valuing the heart of God. It was King David's strength.

Returning to the Gold Standard

The secret of the ministry of Jesus is in the relationship He has with His Father. His primary mission was to reveal Him by displaying His nature and His will. Jesus is the will of God. In doing so, He made startling statements like: *"The Son can do nothing of Himself, but what He sees the Father do...the Son also does in like manner"* (John 5:19) and *"I speak to the world those things which I heard from Him"* (John 8:26). Jesus put Heaven on a collision course with the orphaned planet called earth. His dependence upon the Father brought forth the reality of His world into this one. This is how He could say, *"The Kingdom of Heaven is at hand!"*

All the acts of Jesus were expressions of His Father for all humanity to see. Previous to this all humankind saw the devastating nature of sin, and the consequences for such actions. But Jesus came and furnished the one missing element—the Father. The writer of Hebrews called Jesus the exact representation of His Father's nature (see Heb. 1:3). The life of Jesus is the most complete and accurate revelation of the Father ever seen in this world. Jesus said, *"If you've seen me you've seen my Father"* (John 14:9). It is still true. It is the heart of this perfect Father to give life to humankind (see John 10:10) and destroy all the works of the destroyer (see 1 John 3:8). The Holy Spirit is the one who reveals the heart of the Father to and through us (see John 16:12-15).

The Father's Business

Some things that were so practical for Jesus have become so very abstract to us. This ought not to be. Doing only what the Father is doing is one of the more important areas of life that has been crippled by this tendency to over spiritualize what was quite natural. The following are a few of the ways that I have been able to begin to experience and understand as ways to know what the Father is doing. (Perhaps our bracelets should be changed from WWJD to WIFD—what is Father doing.)

Direct word: There is little doubt that Jesus heard directly from the Father about what He wanted Jesus to do in a particular situation. My personal belief is that much of that direction came in the nights Jesus spent in prayer that preceded the days of ministry. But it is also true that the Holy Spirit who always rested upon Him revealed in the moment what the Father wanted from Him. Learning the many ways that God speaks helps us to be more in tune with this possibility.

Seeing faith in another: One of the more encouraging possibilities that Jesus displayed is the fact that He didn't always seem to know what to do ahead of time, but got His direction by seeing faith in another person. To me, this means that sometimes I can receive direction by seeing the heart response of another to the Holy Spirit's work in them. Faith can exist in a person only through the work of God. So it stands to reason that I can see what the Father is doing by observing the faith in others. But if I'm not familiar with the realm of faith in me, it will be harder to see it in another. The centurion is a great example of this. Jesus was stunned by the faith he saw in that man and responded to his request by releasing the word to heal his servant. *"Now when Jesus heard this, He marveled and said to those who were following, 'Truly I say to you, I have not found such great faith with anyone in Israel'"* (Matt. 8:10). Jesus released the reality of the Kingdom to this man according to his faith. *"And Jesus said to the centurion, 'Go; it shall be done for you as you have believed.' And the servant was healed that very moment"* (Matt. 8:13).

Using our own faith: Often we are unclear as to the specific will of God in a situation. The direction of the Father is not always clear to me. In these situations, it is possible to find the will of God through our own faith as we respond to the revealed will of God in His Word. We sometimes make the mistake of hoping God will come to us and make things clear, when it rests upon us to activate faith and pursue. Many get paralyzed in ministry through their own inactivity. Again, much of what we need in life will be brought to us, but much of what we hunger for will have to be pursued. Abiding faith pursues the will of God until it is found. We will always fall short in this miracle realm if we only respond to the things that become perfectly clear. Some of the greatest breakthroughs I've ever seen came as we responded to a slight impression or an idea of what God might be doing. Our own faith will take us into the discovery of what the Father is doing.

The Outcome

John the Baptist saw the dove come upon Jesus and remain. There is no record of anyone else seeing the dove. Yet everyone saw the result of the dove's presence: both in purity and power, displayed to reveal the heart of God for this orphaned planet.

As the Holy Spirit revealed the Father's will to Jesus, so He reveals the Father's heart to us. And His Presence and power reveal the Father through us. Revealing His will is revealing Him.

Jesus became the ultimate revelation of the will of God on earth. But it's not just through what He accomplished. It is through His relentless and consistent hosting of the Dove.

Giving place to the Presence of God as our greatest joy and treasure is not a trick we use to get miracles. But the Father cannot be adequately represented without miracles. They are essential in revealing His nature.

We make the distinction between the natural and the supernatural. Those are the two realms we live in. But God only has one realm: the natural. It's all natural for Him.

9

Releasing the Dove

It's hard to put into words how moved I am by the story of the Holy Spirit resting upon Jesus like a dove—and remaining. A holy jealousy gets stirred up in me: a jealousy to live in the reality that Jesus lived in. Seeing what is possible through His example has freed me to hunger for what I know is within reach. It has been a growing experience for the last many years, one that continues to progress. Hunger prevails.

Jesus doesn't always tell us what to pursue. Some things only become a part of our lives because we see the ways of God and pursue accordingly. Earlier in this book, I discussed this reality in another context: Jesus didn't teach people to touch His clothing to get well. They observed the nature of God working through Him and responded to what they saw that was available through that example. We can now use the same principle to see what Jesus carried continuously that really set the precedent for how each of us is to live.

We do well to pursue according to His commands. But romance is no longer romance when it is commanded. Some things must be pursued only because they are there. Moses was able to distill the cry of his heart in this simple prayer: *"Let me know Your ways that I may know You"* (Exod. 33:13). Discovering His ways is the invitation to come to Him and know Him in the way revealed. Revelations of His nature are invitations to experience Him. As He reveals His nature to us through the moving of the Holy Spirit, He will often leave us without command. Instead, He longs to discover what is actually in our hearts, as it is in the nature of the heart in love to always respond to the open door for encounter.

The Dove and the Disciples

The Holy Spirit couldn't live in the disciples until they were born again, which couldn't happen until Jesus had died and was raised from the dead. But even though the Spirit of God wasn't in the twelve, He was with the twelve.

> *…The Spirit of truth, whom the world cannot receive, because it does not see Him or know Him, but you know Him because He abides with you and will be in you* (John 14:17).

He said to them: you know Him. This is amazing to me as they were not yet born again. They had a measure of relationship with the Holy Spirit before they were born again.

Sometimes you don't get to know a person until you work with them. That is certainly the setting Jesus created for His disciples. They were to develop a relationship with the Holy Spirit in ministry that would later set them up for the most amazing promotion imaginable: they would become the dwelling place of God on earth.

Jesus was the perfect teacher. His time with the twelve was critical for many reasons. One reason is that during those times He gave practical instruction for the rest of their lives. Both by His instruction and His example He revealed the priority of this wonderful adventure with God the Holy Spirit. But in all honestly, some of Jesus' instruction seems extremely abstract to me and somewhat hard to understand.

Sometimes lessons seem impractical to us because we live in a different atmosphere than when the lesson was given. Having Jesus illustrate how to protect the Presence of the dove, for example, is much more practical when the evidence of that Presence is witnessed moment by moment by the disciples for over three years. When we grow up in an environment where little Presence is displayed, we don't always understand what Jesus taught. The atmosphere created by His manifest Presence and lifestyle contributes amazingly to a lesson being given. Having said that, we are in a season of increased Presence and power: all of this is changing for us. And I'm thankful. As a result, some of the things that have been hidden from us in the Scriptures are now being revealed because we have a place to put them.

Ready or Not, Here We Come

After giving a commission to the 70 disciples, Jesus sent them out in pairs to their hometowns. Interestingly, He considered them to be fully prepared. If truth be told, in most of our churches this group of unqualified people wouldn't be allowed to be ushers or to direct traffic, let alone head up evangelistic campaigns. (I'm of the opinion that we often over train our people until they become spiritually muscle bound.) He sent them out, saying

Carry neither moneybag, knapsack, nor sandals; and greet no one along the road. But whatever house you enter, first say, "Peace to this house." And if a son of peace is there, your peace will rest on it; if not, it will return to you (Luke 10:4).

First of all, notice He sent them out without provisions. No money, no hotel reservations, no rented auditoriums, nothing—just a geographical direction and a shove. One of the things I tried to do for my children is to take care of every possible problem ahead of time so they would be successful. Jesus didn't. He intentionally sent them in over their heads. They stepped into situations where they would need each other (sent out in pairs) and they would need to discover the direction of the Spirit of God, as a team. The goal wasn't for them to have powerful meetings at home, even though they did. The goal was for them to learn to work with the Holy Spirit, who was with them. Jesus was interested in connecting them to the process of hosting the Presence more than He was interested in the outcome of meetings. He was raising up a company of people upon whom the Holy Spirit could also rest and remain.

Many of the lessons we need to learn can only be learned in serving others. The end result was they had powerful meetings at home, which is the most difficult place to be successful in ministry. As Jesus had already noted, *"Truly I say to you, no prophet is welcome in his hometown"* (Luke 4:24). One of the reasons it's so important to learn ministry at home is because of the value of serving where there is no honor. We must not become addicted to the praises of men. If we don't live by their praises, we'll not die by their criticisms. But this was only possible if they first learned the place of the Holy Spirit in the endeavor.

The second thing to take note of is what Jesus told them to do once they found a place to stay. They were to let their peace come upon that household. Is that merely a command to greet people with the word shalom? I doubt it. That lesson could have been taught with much less fanfare. I personally don't believe they really understood this instruction until later in their story. Regardless, they were to release peace, and then interestingly take it back if there was no one there who was worthy (see Matt. 10:13). Luke's Gospel reads that peace would automatically come back to them.

Peace, the Person

The world thinks of peace as the absence of something: a time without war, a time without noise, or a time without conflict. For a believer, Peace is a person—the presence of someone. Our ability to respond to this command of Jesus to release peace over a household is central in His instruction for ministry. It is tied directly to our ability to recognize the Presence of the Holy Spirit. It's hard to release with any consistency what you're not aware of. Consciousness of Presence will always increase our impact when it comes to influencing the world around us.

So much of what we do is done out of ministry principles instead of out of the Presence. One of the mysteries of life is that a primary role of a believer is the stewardship of a person, the Abiding Presence, who is the Holy Spirit—the dove that remains. He is a person, not an it. When we reduce the joy of knowing God to the principles that bring breakthrough, we cheapen the journey. Those who desire principles above Presence seek a kingdom without a king.

Jesus is called the Prince of Peace in Scripture. The Holy Spirit is the Spirit of Christ, the person of peace. And that Peace that is a person is the actual atmosphere of Heaven. That is why peace is like a double-edged sword: it is calming and wonderful for the believer, but highly destructive and invasive for the powers of darkness. *"The God of peace will soon crush Satan under your feet"* (Rom. 16:20). That's quite an assignment given to His followers: release the person of peace when you enter a home, for in doing so, you will release the Presence that is the actual atmosphere of

Heaven to yielded hearts while at the same time undermining the powers of darkness that are at work in that home. For that atmosphere is expressed through the person of the Holy Spirit. For Jesus, this was Ministry 101.

What God Longs For

For God, miracles are as simple as breathing. No effort is required. Because the Spirit of the resurrected Christ lives within us, miracles are expected. But that is not where His desires are focused for us. He wants our hearts. And while there are many expressions of a surrendered heart, He looks for those who will trust Him. Remember, without faith it is impossible to please Him (see Heb. 11:6). Trust is the issue.

To honor Him fully, we have to live in such a way that unless God shows up, what we are attempting to do is bound to fail. This kind of abandonment was the nature of Jesus' life on earth and is now the nature of the believing believer. This is how we are "co-missioned" into this assignment. He said, "Go into a city. Find a place to stay. Don't bring any money. Don't take enough clothing that you can take care of yourself for extended periods of time. Make yourself vulnerable in your abandonment to My purposes, so that unless I show up to provide and direct, it will not work."

This is a context that Jesus gave the disciples in which to live safely as sheep that wolves would like to devour. You would think that becoming vulnerable to risk would be the most unsafe place to be. But this Kingdom works differently. Just as we are exalted by humbling ourselves, and we live by dying, so in this Kingdom we are the safest when we are the most vulnerable to danger because of our "yes" to His assignment. The frontlines of battle are really the safest place to be. David missed out on this truth in his greatest failure.

Then it happened in the spring, at the time when kings go out to battle . . . David stayed at Jerusalem. Now when evening came David arose from his bed and walked around on the roof of the king's house, and from the roof he saw a woman bathing; and the woman was very beautiful in appearance. So David sent and inquired about the woman. And one said, *"Is this not Bathsheba, the daughter of Eliam, the wife of Uriah the Hittite?"* David sent messengers and took her, and when she came to him, he lay with her (see 2 Sam. 11:1-4).

David lost the battle with his eyes, which opened the door for him to lose the battle over his heart, all because he was not in the battle he was born for. It was the season for kings to go out to war. In this season, war would have been a safer place than on his rooftop.

It would be foolish to think the danger of frontlines kind of ministry isn't real. But when the manifest presence of God is with you in your assignment, dangerous places become safe. And the measure we are aware of our need for Him is usually the measure we become aware of Him. It really is all about the Presence. It's about hosting Him. This is what the 70 discovered. Neither their ignorance nor lack of experience disqualified them. They had been sent by One who was going with them.

True Provision

My idea of protection is quite a bit different from God's. I would make sure all the needed arrangements for the trip were taken care of—the contacts, the meeting places, the finances, and sufficient training. I would have also sent about ten people or so to each city to make sure they could minister more effectively. I am constantly amazed at how differently Jesus thinks. He sent them on a journey that was fully prepared, but not in the ways that often matter to me. It was fully prepared because God would go with them. Two people would be enough: they would benefit from the principle of unity, but not fall to the possible conflict that the twelve spies had who spied out the land in Moses' day. Too many opinions easily undermine the purposes of God. Two spies brought back a good report. I'm not saying that traveling in pairs is the only model for ministry. I'm saying that Jesus sent them fully prepared in ways we don't always recognize—God would go with them in their assignment to release peace on a house, heal the sick, raise the dead, etc. Jesus made sure that they stayed Holy Spirit centered. They were prepared the best way possible. They saw Jesus do it, and He commissioned them to an assignment that required them to stay dependent on the Holy Spirit.

As stated, I would have provided all the natural things they needed. Jesus provided the direction and the Presence as seen in the power and authority given to them. What He gave them insures the natural provisions will be there because the Holy Spirit is at work. This is the concept that Jesus taught the multitudes in Matthew 6:33, *"Seek first the kingdom of God...and all these things will be added."* His Kingdom works entirely on the first things first principle. The provision of the Lord is not just food on the table. The supernatural provision of the Lord is divine protection and full impact in our assignment. That is the whole issue: Giving up the reins of being in control of my life to become truly Holy Spirit empowered and directed. His commission was to go learn how the Holy Spirit moves. Go learn His ways.

Noah's Prophecy

A rather surprising place in Scripture to find Jesus' lesson for His disciples is in the story of Noah and the flood. There's one part of the story that illustrates in an Old Testament context what Jesus would train His disciples to do.

So it came to pass, at the end of forty days, that Noah opened the window of the ark which he had made. Then he sent out a raven, which kept going to and fro until the waters had dried up from the earth. He also sent out from himself a dove, to see if the waters had receded from the face of the ground. But the dove found no resting place for the sole of her foot, and she returned into the ark to him, for the waters were on the face of the whole earth. So he put out his hand and took her, and drew her into the ark to himself (Genesis 8:6-9).

I remind you that the dove represents the Holy Spirit in Scripture. This is especially clear in the story of Jesus' water baptism. And here in the story of Noah we find an interesting description of Noah's connection with the dove. There is no other animal that received the same attention or had the implied bond with Noah as did this dove.

The dove was released because she would look for a resting place. When she didn't find a place to rest, she returned to Noah and the ark. That is the picture given of the release of the Holy Spirit through the disciples as they go into someone's home. The implication is that the Holy Spirit is still looking for places to rest— and those places are people. When the dove couldn't find a place to rest, she returned to Noah, the sender. Once again consider Jesus' words concerning their release of peace to a home. If there's no one there that will host this Presence well, *"it will return to you"* (Luke 10:6). When the dove could find no place to rest, the dove came back. Noah put out his hand and brought the dove back to himself. It is interesting phrasing: "from himself" and "to himself." This is an Old Testament glimpse into New Testament ministry.

So he waited yet another seven days; and again he sent out the dove from the ark. The dove came to him toward evening, and behold, in her beak was a freshly picked olive leaf. So Noah knew that the water was abated from the earth (Genesis 8:10, 11).

The dove was released again, but the dove returned giving Noah a progress report. God designed the ark in such a way that there were no windows, except the one in the roof from which to release the dove. Noah was only to look heavenward and rely on the information he received from the dove. The waters were receding from the earth.

Then he waited yet another seven days, and sent out the dove; but she did not return to him again (Genesis 8:12).

The next time he released the dove it didn't return. I believe for most of us this lesson is abstract because we receive so little teaching and experience in learning to recognize the Presence of God. Most would never know in a ministry situation if the dove was released, let alone if He came back. It would be really tough to know if the Holy Spirit that was released from us is now resting upon someone. I state this not to shame anyone but to create hunger for what is legally our privilege and responsibility. We are to know the ways and Presence of the Holy Spirit so we can cooperate with Him in a way that changes the world around us. This is true ministry.

Finding the Worthy

Part of the instruction Jesus gave the 70 was to find those who were worthy to release His peace upon. The whole of Scripture teaches that God doesn't look at the outward appearance of a person. He looks at the heart. This was evidenced in the story of the prophet Samuel looking for a new king for Israel. He had all of Jesse's sons pass before him for examination. In the natural, the prophet found the perfect candidate. But God said no. After looking at all of them, Samuel asked if there was another son who wasn't present. They said yes and went to get David, who was watching his father's sheep. God saw his heart and said he was the one.

David wasn't treated the same as the rest of his brothers. His own father Jesse didn't consider him a possible choice to become king. I'm not sure if this was a simple oversight, or if something else was going on. David spoke of being conceived in sin. *"Behold, I was brought forth in iniquity, and in sin my mother conceived me"* (Ps. 51:5). It is possible that David was the child of another wife of his father Jesse, or possibly even an affair, which would make him the half-brother to the rest. Regardless, neither his father nor his brothers would have chosen him. But God saw his heart and chose him to be the next king.

How do you tell if someone is worthy? The upstanding citizens of the community were not always His first choice. More often than not, it was the demon possessed, the tax collectors, the harlots, etc., who were all considered worthy of a touch from God. I have watched this mystery for years and must admit this is one of the most wonderful and mystifying things about God's choice of a person. God stated that He chose Israel because they were the least of all. This applies to individuals, too.

Consider this: it's obvious that Jesus didn't expect his disciples to know who was worthy when they walked into the house; otherwise, He would have had them release the Presence of the Holy Spirit only when they found the worthy. In other words, they would not have needed the additional instruction to take back the peace if there were any natural indication of who was worthy. They could only know who was worthy by their response to the Holy Spirit—did He rest upon them? Were they responsive to the person of the Holy Spirit or not? Or did the Holy Spirit return to the sender? That is what constitutes worth. It's how they respond to the dove. Amazing.

Great sinners have lost their innocence in so many areas of their lives. But for most of them, there remains deep in their hearts an innocence as it pertains to the Holy Spirit Himself. For most caught in deep sin, this part of the heart is still virgin territory. I've seen it so many times. The most corrupt, the most immoral and deceptive, are changed in a moment when the Holy Spirit comes upon them. Under all the callousness caused by sin was a place of deep tenderness. It is a place that none of us can see without help from the Holy Spirit. Amazingly, their hearts responded to

God when He showed up. It's the ones Jesus referred to when He said, *"Her sins, which are many, have been forgiven, for she loved much; but he who is forgiven little, loves little."* (Luke 7:47) And it's that response that declares they are worthy of the dove.

Conversely, it is often those who have been overexposed to the things of God that actually build a resistance to Him. Overexposure often happens when a person hears much teaching from the Word but doesn't come to a place of total surrender. This was the issue with the Pharisees. The ones who were the most trained to recognize the Messiah when He came missed Him altogether. Total surrender draws us into encounters with God that keep us tender. Without that element, we become hardened to the very word that was given to transform us. It would be similar to the way a vaccination is made. We are exposed to small portions of a particular disease, which in turn causes our body to build a resistance. Jesus is not to be tried in small portions. He is to be surrendered to completely and wholeheartedly. Anything less will often have the opposite result than what He desired for us.

This is a fascinating venture for sure: finding those who are responsive to the Holy Spirit. I know that I've not always responded to Him well. Even now it feels like a lifelong goal to learn to let Him lead in the dance.

Abiding—Being Conscious of Him

In Heaven there are no thoughts void of God. He is the light, the life, and the heart of His world. Heaven is filled with perfect confidence and trust in God. On the other hand, this world is filled with mistrust and chaos. We will always release the reality of the world we are most aware of. Living aware of God is an essential part of the command to abide in Him. Brother Lawrence of the 1600s illustrated this theme remarkably well. It is presented in the book *The Practice of the Presence of God*. It was said of him that there was no difference between his times of prayer and his times working in the kitchen. His awareness of God and His communion with Him were the same in either role.

Living with a continual awareness of Him has got to be a supreme goal for anyone who understands the privilege of hosting Him. He is the Holy Spirit, making holiness a huge part of the focus of our lives. Yet He is as good as He is holy. I get concerned when people have the holiness ambition without discovering the cornerstone of our theology: God is good. I have learned that all my ambition, discipline, and deeply felt repentance had little effect on my life as it pertains to holiness. A holy lifestyle has become the natural result of delighting in the One who is holy—the One who accepts me as I am. All the sweaty efforts have not changed anything in my life worth mentioning, except to make me prideful and miserable. I wish I had discovered this aspect of the Christian life much earlier in my walk with the Lord. It certainly would have saved me years of frustration.

Developing an Awareness of God

Every believer is aware of God, but not always at a conscious level. Developing this awareness is one of the most important aspects of our life in Christ. He is called, "God with us." Knowing Him that way is essential to our development.

A pilot friend of mine once told me of a test they give to pilots in training. They put the trainee in a flight simulator that is able to recreate the atmosphere of an actual plane at a high altitude. Pilots must be able to recognize if there is a systems failure on the plane. For example, a warning goes off when the oxygen levels get too low. The backup oxygen is then used to keep everyone alive. But what do you do if the system that is to warn you of impending danger fails? And that is the point of the test. They've discovered that every person's body reacts differently to diminishing oxygen levels. One person's leg muscle may twitch while another will have the hair on his arms stand up. It really is that diverse. The one who runs the simulator duplicates the atmosphere of a plane flying at a high altitude. They then slowly cause the levels of oxygen to diminish. The pilot is then to write down any sensation they feel in their body. And right before they pass out, the levels are restored to normal. When they are through, the pilot has a list of warning signs to help them realize that if while flying, their leg muscle begins to twitch, they know to check the oxygen. Note that without the flight instructor training to turn their attention to the signals their bodies are picking up, these potential pilots would never know anything was happening to them that was out of the ordinary. Certainly, they would never know their bodies were giving them a warning of low oxygen. We often live in a similar ignorance to the Presence of God.

Every believer experiences God's Presence in some way, but we often remain untrained. This is especially so in a culture that has emphasized cognitive strengths over spiritual and sensual (physical sense) capabilities. For example, our bodies were created with the ability to recognize God's Presence. The psalmist said even his flesh cried out for the living God (see Ps. 84, NKJV). The writer of Hebrews taught that a sign of maturity was the ability to discern good and evil through our senses: *"But solid food is for the mature, who because of practice have their senses trained to discern good and evil"* (Heb. 5:14).

Those who are trained to recognize counterfeit money never study counterfeit money, as the possibilities for making fake money are endless. They immerse themselves in being exposed to the right currency. Then the bad automatically stands out. It's the same with developing our senses to discern good and evil. Immersion in the discovery of God's Presence upon us (the Spirit given without measure) will cause anything contrary to stand out. Generally, my heart can tell when something is right or wrong. But I've had Him speak in a way that only my natural senses could pick up what He was saying or revealing. He does this intentionally to train us as good soldiers in His army to hear in all contexts in which He may be moving or speaking. This makes us capable of being "instant in season and out."

Discover Him Through Affection

The Holy Spirit is such an amazing lover. He is so tender and always near. One of the things I have discovered, almost by accident, is that whenever I turn my affection toward Him, He begins to manifest upon me. Learning how to release affection to Him and then recognizing His response is valuable to me beyond words. He comes. And His coming is always wonderful.

It has been a practice of mine for many years now to go to sleep at night with this simple act: release my affection for Him until I sense His Presence rest upon me. Now because I'm interested in sleep, I don't use this time to sing praises or even intercede about some great need. I simply love Him until my heart is warmed by His Presence. If I wake in the night, I resume and turn my heart toward Him again and go to sleep engaged with Him.

It's important to know how life works. When God created everything, *"there was evening and there was morning, one day."* This is repeated many times in Genesis chapter one. The day starts at night. Giving Him our nights is the way to start our day. Many would do better in the daytime if they'd learn to give Him their nights. For many, the torment that is experienced in the night watches would end by this simple action. Start your day at night by giving Him your affection until He warms your heart. Learn to maintain that sense of Presence throughout the night, and it will affect your day.

Returning to an Old Lesson

After His resurrection, Jesus met with His disciples in a room where they were hiding. But it was not a meeting they were planning on. They were hiding because they feared that the religious leaders would kill them next. Jesus either walked through the wall or just appeared in the room. That couldn't have helped their fear issues. Jesus responded to their panic with *"Peace be with you"* (John 20:19). They didn't catch what Jesus made available. When peace is given, it must be received in order to be of benefit. After that, Jesus showed them His hands and His side that they might see the scars of his crucifixion. *"The disciples then rejoiced when they saw the Lord"* (John 20:20). Only after seeing those scars did they realize who He was. He then spoke peace to them again.

Jesus often comes differently than we expect. He did the same to the men on the road to Emmaus (see Luke 24:13-32). They didn't recognize Him, either, even though He opened up the Scriptures to them in a way that caused their hearts to burn. Only after He broke the bread at the dinner table were their eyes opened to know who He was. Both times His followers realized who He was only after He drew their attention to the cross—the scars from the spear in His side and the nails in His hands, and the bread, which spoke of His broken body. Moves of God must have the cross as the central point to maintain their genuineness—keeping first things first. The throne is the center of His Kingdom, and on His throne sits the Lamb of God. The blood sacrifice will be honored and celebrated throughout eternity. While it is the resurrection that correctly illustrates and empowers the Christian life, it is the cross that brings us there. There is no resurrection without the cross.

"Peace be with you." Jesus returned to the lesson He gave them in their first commission in Matthew 10:8-12. He taught them to release peace when they enter a house. Jesus calmed a storm with peace. *"Then He arose and rebuked the wind, and said to the sea, 'Peace, be still!' And the wind ceased and there was a great calm"* (Mark 4:39, NKJV). But it was the storm He slept in. We have authority over any storm we can sleep in. You

have to have peace to give it away. Abiding in peace makes us a threat to any storm.

After Jesus showed them the scars, they believed. He spoke peace to them again, as He is the God of the second chance. They apparently were open to it this time because He followed it with the greatest commission anyone has ever received. *"So Jesus said to them again, "Peace be with you; as the Father has sent Me, I also send you"* (John 20:21). There it is: as the Father has sent me, I also send you. Stunning. There is no greater call than to walk in the call of Jesus. But if that wasn't enough, we come to the part that makes it possible. *"And when He had said this, He breathed on them and said to them, 'Receive the Holy Spirit'"* (John 20:22).

If Jesus were to say that as the Father sent Him, He also sends us, and then follow it by having a banquet for the poor, we'd emphasize feeding the poor as the primary ministry of Jesus we are to walk in. If He followed this great commission with a two hour-long worship service, we'd say that that was the primary function we are to walk in. Whatever action follows the command will be emphasized as primary: that is, unless it is abstract, which is the case in this situation. Because it is something so unusual, this action of Jesus gets lost in the long list of activities that only God can do—release the Spirit of God. I'd like to suggest that Jesus was modeling the nature of all ministry in this one act. To do what He did involves releasing the dove (Holy Spirit) until He finds places (people) to rest upon. In this one act, Jesus summarizes the life of those who follow Him in the greatest commission—as the Father sent me, I also send you—now release the Spirit of God.

Power and Authority

Jesus had already given His disciples power and authority while He was still on the earth. They cooperated with the Spirit while on the "mission trips" as well as during the earthly ministry of Jesus. Interestingly, what He gave them would not carry through after His death and resurrection. He brought them into His experience and enabled them to function under the umbrella of His authority and power, which they did well. Now they would have to have their own experience with God to have these two necessary ingredients.

When the disciples received the Holy Spirit in John 20, they were born again. They received a commission from God that was reaffirmed and expanded in Matthew:

> *Go therefore and make disciples of all the nations, baptizing them in the name of the Father and the Son and the Holy Spirit, teaching them to observe all that I commanded you; and lo, I am with you always, even to the end of the age* (Matthew 28:19-20).

Following this experience they were commanded not to leave Jerusalem until they were clothed with power from Heaven. *"And behold, I am sending forth the promise of My Father upon you; but you are to stay in the city until you are clothed with power from on high"* (Luke 24:49). Authority comes with the commission, but power comes with the encounter. They were commanded not to leave until they had their encounter with the Spirit of God. In Matthew 28, they received authority, but in Acts 2, they received power. To this day this is true: authority comes from the commission, and power comes from the encounter. And while these two elements seem to have their primary focus on ministry, they are first the essential elements for our engaging the Holy Spirit for relationship. Power and authority introduce us to the nature of the Holy Spirit with a primary focus on hosting His Presence. Ministry should flow out of the relationship with the person who lives in us for our sakes, but rests upon us for the sake of others.

Releasing His Presence

There are probably countless ways of releasing the presence of God. I am acquainted with four that are intentional.

WORD

Jesus used this method frequently. He only said what His Father was saying. That means every word He spoke had its origins in the heart of the Father. When He spoke His most confusing message, the crowds abandoned Him en masse. This all happened in John 6. In this message, He spoke of how the people would have to eat His flesh and drink His blood to have any part in Him. Never before had Jesus taught on something so grotesque. To the listener He was speaking of cannibalism. We know that wasn't His intent. But we live after the fact. And the most amazing part to me is that Jesus didn't bother explaining what He meant. There's probably not a teacher or pastor alive that wouldn't have made sure the people understood what He was referring to, especially when we saw the crowd murmuring and ultimately leaving. Yet it served His purpose as they intended to make Him king by force. When He asked His disciples if they were leaving, too, Peter responded, *"Lord, to whom shall we go? You have words of eternal life"* (John 6:68). To my point of view, Peter was saying, "We don't understand your teaching more than those who left. But what we do know is that whenever you talk, we come alive inside. When you talk, we find out why we're alive!"

In just a few verses earlier, Jesus explained an especially important part of the Christian life of ministry when He said, *"The words that I have spoken to you are spirit and are life"* (John 6:63). Jesus is the word made flesh. But when He spoke, the word became Spirit. That is what happens whenever we say what the Father is saying. We've all experienced this: we are in a troubling situation, and someone walks in the room and says something that changes the atmosphere of the entire room. It wasn't merely because they came in with a great idea. They spoke something that became material—a substance that changed the atmosphere. What happened? They spoke something timely and purposeful. They said what the Father was saying. Words become spirit.

Words are the tools with which God created the world. The spoken word is also central to creating faith in us (see Rom. 10:17). His spoken word is creative in nature. Saying what the Father is saying releases the creative nature and Presence of God into a situation to bring His influence and change.

ACT OF FAITH

His Presence accompanies His acts. Faith brings a substantial release of Presence, which is visible time after time in Jesus' ministry. An act of faith is any action on the outside that demonstrates the faith on the inside. For example, I've told people to run on a severely injured ankle or leg. As soon as they do, they are healed. How? The Presence is released in the action. That is something I would never do out of the principle of faith. I am only willing to give that direction out of the Presence. Many leaders make a huge mistake at this point. I will never require someone to put themselves at risk out of a principle. If I am experiencing what appears to be a roadblock in my walk with Christ, I will at times require a bold act of myself out of principle—but never someone else.

PROPHETIC ACT

This is a unique facet of the Christian life as it requires an action that by appearance has no connection to the desired outcome. Whereas stepping on an injured ankle is connected to the desired outcome—a healed ankle—a prophetic act has no connection. A great example would be when Elisha was told about a borrowed axe head that fell into the river. It says, *"He cut off a stick and threw it in there, and made the iron float"* (2 Kings 6:6). You can throw sticks in the water all day long and never make an axe head swim.

The act is seemingly unrelated. The strength of the prophetic act is that it comes from the heart of the Father. It is a prophetic act of obedience that has a logic outside human reasoning.

I've seen this happen many times when someone is wanting a miracle. I've had them move from where they were sitting and stand in the aisle of the church. It wasn't because there was more power of the Holy Spirit in the aisle. It's because it was a prophetic act that would release the presence of the Holy Spirit upon them. Jesus operated in this many times. He once told a blind man to wash in the pool of Siloam (see John 9:7). There is no healing power in the pool. The miracle was released in the act of going and washing—both logically unrelated to the desired outcome.

TOUCH

The laying on of hands is one of the primary doctrines of the church specifically referred to as a doctrine of Christ (see Heb. 6:1-2). It was a practice in the Old Testament, too. The priest laid his hands on a goat to symbolically release the sins of Israel on that goat that would then be released into the wilderness. The laying on of hands upon the goat was to release something that would help Israel come into their purpose. It was also used to impart authority, as in the case of Moses and his elders. The apostle Paul laid his hands on Timothy to release apostolic commissioning. In Acts, hands were laid on people for the release of the Holy Spirit upon them (see Acts 8:18). The point is this: laying hands on people is a tool that God uses to release the reality of His world, His Presence, upon another.

Non-intentional

Besides the intentional release of His presence, there are countless ways of His presence being released that are not intentional on our part. Yet by cooperating with Him, they become normal.

SHADOW

Peter's shadow is one of the great stories about the overflow of Presence upon a person. There is no indication that this was directed or expected by Peter. But people learned to access what rested upon him. Our shadow will always release whatever overshadows us. Being a resting place of the Spirit makes both the shadow and the anointed cloth/articles of clothing items of great power in our lives. I don't believe this principle has anything to do with our shadow. It has to do with the proximity to the anointing. Things become possible through us that have nothing to do with our faith. They have everything to do with who is resting upon us—who we're giving place to. In this context more good things happen by accident than ever used to happen on purpose.

COMPASSION

I list this as non-intentional because it comes from within, almost like a volcano. It often says that Jesus was moved by compassion and healed someone. Being willing to love people with the love of Christ brings the miraculous to the forefront. Often people confuse compassion and sympathy. Sympathy gives attention to a person in need, but cannot deliver them. Compassion, on the other hand, comes to set them free. Sympathy is the counterfeit of compassion.

CLOTHING

This operates through the same principle as the shadow mentioned above. The manifest Presence of God upon a person makes unimaginable things possible. His Presence saturates cloth.

WORSHIP

This has an unusual effect on our surroundings. We know that He inhabits our praise (see Ps. 22:3). It stands to reason that

Presence is released. Atmosphere is changed. In fact, the atmosphere of Jerusalem came about in part because of worship. *"We hear them in our own tongues speaking of the mighty deeds of God"* (Acts 2:11). Such praise contributed to an atmospheric shift over an entire city where the spiritual blindness was lifted, followed by 3,000 souls being saved.

I've seen this myself when we've rented a particular facility for church services, only to have the people who use it afterward comment on the Presence that remains. A friend of mine used to take people onto the streets in San Francisco many years ago. They met with heavy resistance. But when he realized that when God arises, His enemies are scattered, he strategically used this approach for ministry (see Ps. 68). He split his team into two. One half went out to worship, and the other half would minister to people. The police told him that when he is on the streets, crime stops. This is an amazing result from a dove being released over a part of the city. The atmosphere changes as the Presence is given His rightful place.

The Ultimate Assignment

I can't think of any greater privilege than to carry the Presence of the Holy Spirit into this world and then look for open doors to release Him. I once had a prophet friend tell me, "If you know of a church that you think I should go to, let me know, and I'll go there." He was basically saying to me, "You have favor in my eyes. And if there is a church that you want me to go to, I'll show them the same favor that I would show to you." Somehow that is the nature of this supreme call. As we steward His Presence properly, in relationship, He will allow us the increasing privilege of releasing His Presence into various situations and people's lives in ministry. He will show them the same favor He has shown us.

10

THE PRACTICAL SIDE OF HIS PRESENCE

I'm not sure when it happened, or even how it happened, but somewhere in church history the focus of our corporate gatherings became the sermon. I'm sure the change was subtle and was even justified: it's the high value we have for the Word of God. But to me, it's not a good enough reason. That is not to devalue the Scriptures. It's just that the physical presence of a Bible should never become the replacement of the Spirit of God upon His people.

Israel camped around the tabernacle of Moses, which housed the Ark of the Covenant. This is where the Presence of God dwelt. This was the absolute center of life for the nation. It was practical for them. Israel camped around the Presence of God, while the church often camps around a sermon. Somehow we must adjust whatever is necessary to rediscover the practical nature of the Presence of God being central to all we do and are.

It's been said of the early church that 95 percent of their activities would have stopped had the Holy Spirit been removed from them. But it is also stated that 95 percent of the modern church's activities would continue as normal because there is so little recognition of His Presence. Thankfully, these percentages are changing, as God has been retooling us for His last days thrust of Presence and harvest. But we have ways to go.

Being Presence-centered as a church, a family, and as an individual must be put on the front burner again. It is the heart of God for us, as it helps us mature in that all-important issue of trust.

With All Our Hearts

One of the most arrogant thoughts to ever enter the mind is that the Presence of God isn't practical. Such a lie keeps us from discovering His nearness. He is the author of the book, the designer of life, and the inspiration for the song. He is the ultimate in practicality.

Living conscious of His Presence with us is one of the most essential parts to this life. His name is Emmanuel, which means God with us. The God with us lifestyle is one we inherited from Jesus. We must live it with the same priority of Presence to have the same impact and purpose as He did.

Trust in the Lord with all your heart and do not lean on your own understanding. In all your ways acknowledge Him, and He will make your paths straight (Proverbs 3:5-6).

Trust will take us beyond understanding into realms that only faith can discover. Trust is built on interaction, and the resulting discovery of His nature, which is good and perfect in every way. We don't believe because we understand. We understand because we believe. Understanding we receive in this manner is the "renewed mind." Discovering a fuller expression of God's nature and Presence is exponentially increased with this simple element called trust.

To acknowledge Him is the natural result when we trust Him. The one we trust above our own existence is to be recognized in every aspect and part of life. The word, acknowledge, actually means to know. It is an unusually big word in Scripture, with a broad range of meanings. But the thing that stands out to me the most is that this word often points to the realm of personal experience. It is bigger than head knowledge. It is beyond concepts alone. It is a knowing through encounter. In fact, Genesis 4:1 it says, *"And Adam knew Eve his wife; and she conceived, and bare Cain"* (KJV). Obviously, a word of this nature is more than an idea. It is deep interaction.

The Presence Journey

Trust makes His Presence more discoverable. He becomes much more tangible to the one who looks to Him with reliance and expectation. As I've mentioned, my strongest tool for discovering God's Presence is my affection for Him. Even so, He is the initiator. He is the great lover of humanity and chooses to draw near in these glorious moments. I cannot imagine life without the wonderful privilege of loving Him. He draws near. So very near.

This passage from Proverbs 3 indicates the one who trusts Him should acknowledge Him or recognize until knowing and encountering Him. My personal loose paraphrase would go something like this: "In every part of your life recognize Him until it becomes a personal encounter with Him. He'll make life better." I never like the idea of presenting formulas that cheapen our walk with the Lord, and certainly don't mean to imply that in this case. Yet acknowledging God's Presence and encountering Him will certainly make things work better in life. It's a given. The author, designer, and inspiration for life itself is essential to have on board—with full recognition from us.

Many of us have pursued a life of faith for many important reasons. The miracle realm is certainly one of them. Miracles are now a regular part of our lives in numbers I never thought were possible. It is wonderful. But of late I've wondered whether we might not surpass what we've seen in the miraculous if we used our faith to discover the Presence of God as much as we have used it to get breakthrough for miracles. The bottom line: use your faith to discover God's abiding Presence on your life. He never disappoints. The overwhelming outcome is learning to live from the Presence of God toward the issues of life. This Jesus did perfectly.

The Presence of God upon us is due north. When the compass of my heart discovers the Presence of God, everything else falls into place much more easily. And while I may not have the answer I am looking for in every specific area of need, I recognize the Presence that keeps me from the fear and anxiety that blocks my access to answers. Divine order fills the life of the one who has the Presence of God as the priority.

Deep Repentance

Trust is the natural expression of the one in deep repentance. The nature of these two realities is portrayed well in Hebrews 6:1, *"repentance from dead works and of faith toward God."* In this one verse we see the nature of both repentance and faith—from and toward. The picture is of one making an about face, from something and toward something. Here it is from sin toward God Himself. His Presence is discovered in repentance.

Repentance means to change the way we think. Our perspective changes regarding sin and God. With deep sorrow we confess (fully own up to our sin without excuse) and turn to God (upon whom we place our entire trust).

Similar imagery is given in Acts. *"Therefore repent and return, so that your sins may be wiped away, in order that times of refreshing may come from the presence of the Lord"* (Acts 3:19). Note the end result—that times of refreshing may come from the presence of the Lord. In these two verses we see the pattern, the order that God created to lead us to Himself, to His manifest Presence. While we were sinners, God chose us to experience Him in such a way that we were fully restored to our original design, to live in and carry His Presence.

We are either walking in repentance, or we need to repent. Repentance is the lifestyle of being face-to-face with God. If that is missing, I must turn back. I must repent.

Holy Spirit Praying

Perhaps the greatest understatement of this book is that the Presence of God is discovered in prayer. And while that is an obvious truth, many people learn to pray without the Presence, thinking their discipline is what God is looking for. Discipline has an important part in walking with Christ, for sure. But Christianity was never to be known for its disciplines; it was to be known by its passions.

Prayer is the ultimate expression of partnership with God. It is the adventure of discovering and praying His heart. So many spend their life praying to God, when they could be praying with God. This partnership, with its answers and breakthroughs, is supposed to be the source of our fullness of joy.

But you, beloved, building yourselves up on your most holy faith, praying in the Holy Spirit (Jude 20).

With all prayer and petition pray at all times in the Spirit (Ephesians6:18).

One who speaks in a tongue edifies himself (1 Corinthians 14:4).

When we pray anointed prayers, we are praying the heart of God. His heart is being expressed through words, emotion, and decree. Finding the heart of God is a sure way of locking into His Presence. This privilege of co-laboring is a part of the assignment given for those who would give themselves to carry His Presence well.

Praying in tongues brings us edification and personal strength. In that kind of praying the Presence of God washes over us to bring great refreshing. I think it's a bit sad when people emphasize that tongues is the least of the gifts, which seems to give them the right to ignore it while they pursue the greater gifts. If one of my children took the birthday or Christmas gift I gave them and refused to open it because they discerned it was one of lesser value than the others, they'd hear a sermon from me they'd not soon forget. Any gift from God is wonderful, glorious, and extremely necessary to live in His full intentions for us. This particular gift is brilliantly useful for living in the Presence continually.

Creative Expression

One of the great mysteries in life is to see the descendants of the Creator show so little creativity in how we do church and life in general. I don't think that lack comes from people who like to be bored or who like to control things to death. It usually comes from a misunderstanding of who He is and what He is like. People often fear being wrong so much that they fail to try something new, thinking they will displease God. If more people would relax in His goodness, we'd probably give a more accurate expression of the God who is never boring. He is still creative. And it's in our nature to be the same.

During my prayer times I have to have paper and pen with me because of the ideas I get while I'm praying. I used to think it was the devil distracting me from praying. That's because I measured prayer by how much time I spent doing a one-way conversation. God measures prayer through time spent in interaction.

Time in His Presence will release creative ideas. When I spend time with God, I remember phone calls I need to make, projects I long forgot about, and things I had planned to do with my wife or my children. Ideas flow freely in this environment because that's the way He is. I get ideas in the Presence I wouldn't get anywhere else. Insights on how to fix problems or people that need to be affirmed all come in that exchange of fellowship between God and man. We must stop blaming the devil for all those interruptions. (Many of us have too big a devil and too small a God.) And while the enemy of our souls will work to distract us from the Presence, he's often blamed when he is nowhere near because we misunderstand our Father and what He values. When we realize that often it's God interacting with us, we are able to enjoy the process much more and give Him thanks for having concern for these parts of our lives that we might often think are too small for His input. If it matters to you, it matters to Him. These ideas are the fruit of our two-way conversation. But in order to keep from leaving the privilege of interaction with God to work on other things, I write these things down so I can return to my worship and fellowship with Him. The notes I write give me directions I can return to later.

Because God is resting upon us, we should expect new levels of creative ideas with which to impact our world. By referring to creative, I'm not just talking about painting or writing songs, etc.

Creativity is the touch of the Creator on every part of life. It's the need of the accountant and the lawyer as much as it is for the musician and actor. It is to be expected when you're the son or daughter of the Creator, Himself.

Prayer Time, Worship Time

My prayer times are less and less about issues of need, and more and more about discovering this wonderful person who has given Himself so freely and completely to me. I remember hearing Derek Prince speak on this subject about 40 years ago. It impacted me so profoundly. He said if you have ten minutes to pray, take about eight minutes for worship. It's amazing what you can pray for in two minutes.

Worship has become a primary part of life. It's wonderful when it's in the corporate gathering. But it's shallow when it's only corporate. My personal life must be one of continuous worship to experience the transformations that I long for. We always become like the one we worship.

I still believe in prayer and intercession. It is a joy. But my heart has this bent toward the Presence that is bigger than the answers I am seeking. There's a person to be discovered, daily. He must be enjoyed, and discovered yet again. And it's all His idea. I can seek Him only because He found me.

Five-Minute Vacation

One of the more meaningful parts of my life is the five-minute vacations I take. They can happen any time or anywhere. The amount of time I take varies, but the activity does not. For example, if I'm in my office, I'll ask my secretary to hold my calls for a few minutes. I will sit down and generally close my eyes and pray something like this, "God, I'm going to sit here quietly, just to be the object of your love." The flow of His love for us is huge, likened to the water that flows over Niagara Falls—except Niagara is too small. Becoming aware of that love and experiencing that love is wonderful beyond words. It has the side benefit of driving out all fear.

There are only two basic emotions in life: love and fear. Turning my attention toward His love for me only increases my love for Him. It's an unending love fest where I delight in Him as He delights in me, which only increases my delight in Him. He is the ultimate pleasure and must be treasured as such.

Many of us have been raised thinking there was a lot of work in prayer. Actually, I still value that model, but now only when it comes out of the lifestyle of Presence and romance. It is most effective when I'm in love. Discovering His Presence daily is the surest way to stay in love.

I have set the Lord continually before me; because He is at my right hand, I will not be shaken (Psalm 16:8).

This psalm of David is a favorite for a number of reasons. It is a psalm of discovery of Presence. It concludes in verse 11 with *"In Your presence is fullness of joy; in Your right hand there are pleasures forever."* Fullness of joy. Where? In the Presence! There would be more joy in the house if we became more aware of the One who was in the house.

The verse mentioned above is unique because of this one concept—I have set the Lord continually before me. Here the word set means to place, as in to put something in its rightful place. David made it a daily practice to place God right in front of Him. He turned his attention toward God with him until he became aware of Him. David, the one most honored in Scripture as a person of God's Presence said that this was how he did life. Considering the outcome of David's life, I don't think it's a stretch to say this was a secret to David's success in the Presence. He knew that if He didn't turn His attention toward the Lord who was with Him, He would live without due north. He would lack the reference point in his compass that put everything else in life in its place.

Read Until He Speaks

While worship is the number one way that God has used to teach me about His Presence, a very close second would be my encounters with Him through His Word. I love the Scriptures so much. Most of what I have learned about the voice of God has been learned in the reading of His Word. And while I believe in the intense study of Scripture, I mostly read for pleasure. In fact, I always read for pleasure.

God has spoken to me countless times through the years from the pages of His book. It is now a habit to immediately go to His Word when I need direction, comfort, insight or wisdom. If I'm troubled by something, I go to the Psalms. Every emotion is well represented in that book. And I read until I hear my voice in a psalm. Once I hear my heart's cry, I know I have found the place for me to stop and feed. It's probably much like sheep that have found a pasture of bounty to feed from. They just stop and enjoy. That's my life. I stop and feed on the wonderful interaction, the voice, the actual Presence of God that is manifested in and through His Word.

"So faith comes from hearing, and hearing by the word of Christ" (Rom. 10:17). There are two important things I want to point to in this great verse. First is the fact that faith comes from hearing, not from having heard. The second is that faith doesn't necessarily come from hearing the Word. Faith comes from hearing. Our capacity to hear comes from the Word. Being one who hears now is one who is in line for great faith. Our entire life is attached to His voice. Man lives by *"every word that proceeds out of the mouth of God"* (Matt. 4:4).

Community for Communion

God loves the church. He loves the idea, the potential, and everything to do with the church, His Son's body on earth. In fact, He stated that zeal for this house has consumed Him! He has devoted His strength, wisdom, and His intense emotions to this house on earth: His eternal dwelling place.

What I experience with God at home on my own is priceless. I wouldn't trade it for anything in the world. But neither would I trade the amazing moments I've experienced through the years in the gatherings of hundreds or thousands. They are also priceless moments that prepare us for eternity where people from every tribe and tongue will lift up praises to the Lord. This is indescribable joy.

Some things are reserved for the individual. And yet some things are actually too precious to be given to only one. They must be shared with a company of people, a body, the church. And there are aspects of His Presence that will only be experienced in the corporate gathering. The exponential release and discovery of Presence is equal to the size of the group of people united in the purpose of exalting Jesus in praise.

There are times when God will only allow us to recognize His Presence in a crowd. It's not a rejection. He just longs for us to share His joy in the whole.

Building a Personal History

Many have come to me through the years asking for a prayer of impartation, which is the release of a gift for ministry through the laying on of hands, often accompanied by prophecy. It has been one of the great privileges of life to see how God uses both their hunger and the anointing on my life to impact another willing vessel. And while impartation has become rightfully more important in recent years, for some it has become a shortcut to maturity, which really can only be developed through faithful service over time. Getting an instant answer is almost always preferred by those of us raised in this culture of immediate gratification. We sometimes forget: gifts are free; maturity is expensive.

I believe that giving and receiving impartation is such an amazing privilege. But like many, I also have seen it abused. That abuse is probably why many in my parents' generation rejected the concept of impartation altogether. But the testimonies of this great principle are bringing forth undeniable fruit to the glory of God. Learning how to access great anointing on another person's life is a great key to personal breakthrough.

The release of a gift through the laying on of hands is entirely God's doing. We are not vending machines where you put in your request, push a button, and out comes the desired gift. Often someone will tell me that they want twice what I have. Well, so do I! If it were that easy, I would lay hands on myself and pray, "Double it!" Of late, I've been telling people, "I can lay hands on you and impart an anointing into your life as God wills. But I can't give you my history with God."

There is something priceless in a person's life that must be developed and protected at any cost: it's our private history with God. If you make history with God, God will make history through you. This history is created when no one is watching—it's who we are when we are alone. It's seen in the cry of our hearts, how we think, what we pray, and how we value God, Himself. Our lives are shaped when there is no one able to applaud our sacrifice or efforts.

These are the moments that we learn the most about hosting His Presence. It's when there's no one to pray for, no one to serve—that's where the relational boundaries are determined. Am I in this for how God can use me, or am I surrendered because

He is God, and there is no greater honor in life? Jesus had His encounter with the Holy Spirit at His water baptism. A crowd watched. Probably very few, if any, had an idea of what was happening. But it was on the nights on the mountain, when no one was watching, that His greatest breakthroughs came. History was made in Him before history was made through Him. He loved the Father before He could reveal the Father.

11

BAPTISM OF FIRE

John the Baptist was the greatest of all the New Testament prophets. His responsibility, his anointing, and his place in history all put him at the top of the list. Jesus is the one who pointed out this fact in His remarkable affirmation of John in Matthew 11. Over half the chapter was dedicated to his honor.

John had so much going for him: he walked in the Spirit and power of Elijah, he ended Heaven's silence with his cries of the Kingdom of Heaven being at hand, and he was given the privilege to pave the way for the Messiah. Yet according to John, he was lacking one primary ingredient: Jesus' baptism. This desire came to light when Jesus came to John to be baptized in water. John had trouble figuring out how he could baptize Him as Jesus was not the one in need. In the overwhelming contrast with

Jesus' perfection, John realized his need. He confessed his desire with, *"I have need to be baptized by You"* (Matt. 3:14). Interestingly, this all came about right after John had prophesied, *"He will baptize you with the Holy Spirit and fire"* (Matt. 3:11). It was fresh on his mind. That is the context for his confession. John needed and desired the baptism of fire—the baptism in the Holy Spirit. It is this one essential gift from God that makes it possible for *"the one who is least in the kingdom of heaven* [to be] *greater than he"* (Matt. 11:11). John had no access to that baptism. Yet it's that baptism that makes it possible for every New Testament believer to be greater than the greatest of the Old Testament prophets. This is fire at a whole new level. And this fire is Presence.

The Grace Umbrella

Jesus brought the disciples into the authority and power He lived in. As stated earlier, they functioned under the umbrella of His experience, and were deputized as a result. But before He left earth to live at the right hand of the Father, He made sure the disciples knew that the realm they had lived in for three and a half years with Him would never be enough for the days to come. They had to get their own power and authority.

Matthew 28 gives the most complete and well known of the Great Commission passages.

All authority has been given to Me in heaven and on earth. Go therefore and make disciples of all the nations, baptizing them in the name of the Father and the Son and the Holy Spirit, teaching them to observe all that I commanded you; and lo, I am with you always, even to the end of the age (Matthew 28:18-20).

In it Jesus declares that He has all authority, which obviously implies that the devil has none. In that moment, He gives a commission to His followers. The secret of this moment is that authority is given in the commission. He then instructs them to wait in Jerusalem until they are clothed with power from on high.

Just as authority comes in the commission, so power comes in the encounter. We see it in Jesus' life, and so it is for the disciples. And it's no different for us. There is nothing that training, study, or association with the right people can do to make up for this one thing. There is nothing to replace a divine encounter. Everyone must have their own.

Tragically, many stop short of a divine encounter because they're satisfied with good theology. Once a concept is seen in Scripture, it can be shared with others even though there's no personal experience to back it up. True learning comes in the experience, not the concept by itself. Often we can become guilty of only looking for something to happen to us that is on our list of what constitutes a "biblical" encounter with God. The lists of various experiences discovered in Scripture do not contain God; they reveal Him. In other words, He is bigger than His book, and is not limited to doing something for us the exact same way He did for someone else. He continues to be creative, each time revealing the wonder of who He is.

Many fail to realize that what is needed in this pursuit of more is an abandonment to God that attracts something that cannot be explained, controlled, or understood. We must encounter one who is bigger than we are in every possible way until He leaves a mark. It is wonderful, glorious, and scary.

My Story—Glorious, but Not Pleasant

In my personal quest for increased power and anointing in my ministry, I have traveled to many cities, including Toronto. God has used my experiences in such places to set me up for life-changing encounters at home.

Once in the middle of the night, God came in answer to my prayer for more of Him, yet not in a way I had expected. I went from a dead sleep to being wide-awake. Unexplainable power began to pulsate through my body, seemingly just shy of electrocution. It was as though I had been plugged into a wall socket with a thousand volts of electricity flowing through my body. My arms and legs shot out in silent explosions as if something was released through my hands and feet. The more I tried to stop it, the worse it got.

I soon discovered that this was not a wrestling match I was going to win. I heard no voice, nor did I have any visions. This was simply the most overwhelming experience of my life. It was raw power...it was God. He came in response to a prayer I had been praying for months—God, I must have more of you at any cost!

The evening before was glorious. We were having meetings with a good friend and prophet, Dick Joyce. The year was 1995. At the end of the meeting, I prayed for a friend who was having difficulty experiencing God's presence. I told him that I felt God was going to surprise him with an encounter that could come in the middle of the day, or even at 3 A.M. When the power fell on me that night, I looked at the clock. It was 3 A.M., exactly. I knew I had been set up.

For months I had been asking God to give me more of Him. I wasn't sure of the correct way to pray, nor did I understand the doctrine behind my request. All I knew was I was hungry for God. It had been my constant cry day and night.

This divine moment was glorious, but not pleasant. At first I was embarrassed, even though I was the only one who knew I was in that condition. As I lay there, I had a mental picture of me standing before my congregation, preaching the Word as I loved to do. But I saw myself with my arms and legs flailing about as though I had serious physical problems. The scene changed—I was walking down the main street of our town, in front of my favorite restaurant, again arms and legs moving about without control.

I didn't know of anyone who would believe that this was from God. I recalled Jacob and his encounter with the angel of the Lord. He limped for the rest of His life. And then there was Mary, the mother of Jesus. She had an experience with God that not even her fiancée believed, although a visit from an angel helped to change his mind. As a result she bore the Christ-child...and then bore a stigma for the remainder of her days as the mother of the illegitimate child. It was becoming clear; the favor of God sometimes looks different from the perspective of earth than from Heaven. My request for more of God carried a price.

Tears began to soak my pillowcase as I remembered the prayers of the previous months and contrasted them with the scenes that just passed through my mind. At the forefront was the realization that God wanted to make an exchange—His increased presence for my dignity. It's difficult to explain how you know the purpose of such an encounter. All I can say is you just know. You know His purpose so clearly that every other reality fades into the shadows, as God puts His finger on the one thing that matters to Him.

In the midst of the tears came a point of no return. I gladly yielded, crying, More, God. More! I must have more of You at any cost! If I lose respectability and get You in the exchange, I'll gladly make that trade. Just give me more of You!

The power surges didn't stop. They continued throughout the night, with me weeping and praying, More Lord, more, please give me more of You. It all stopped at 6:38 A.M., at which time I got out of bed completely refreshed. This experience continued the following two nights, beginning moments after getting into bed.

Extremes

There are many interesting encounters that God has had with His people throughout the years. It's a mistake to use one as the standard for all. The two most life-changing encounters I've had with God couldn't be more different from one another. Above, I related the story of being electrocuted in His Presence. The other one was so subtle that it would have been as easy to miss as it was to catch. It was because I "turned aside." The Bible says, *"When Moses turned aside...God spoke."* My burning bush was a Scripture that the Holy Spirit highlighted to me. I stopped and considered it, pursuing what God might be saying. That was May of 1979, and I've never been the same since. It started small, much like a seed. But it has been increasing continuously, having tremendous impact for how I think and live. (It was Isaiah 60:1-19, where God showed me the purpose and nature of the church.)

Your encounter with God may stir up a holy jealousy in me; it isn't healthy to judge what God has done in me by comparing it to what He's done for you. In the electrocution experience I mentioned above, I didn't know if I'd ever get out of bed again. It seemed that my circuits were fried and that I had lost the ability to function in life as a normal human being. That, of course, wasn't the case. But I only learned that after the fact: after I said yes to "more at any price."

It's not how extreme an encounter is with God. It's how much of us He apprehends in the experience—and how much of His presence He can entrust to us. Jesus manifested a lifestyle, as a man, that is intensely practical, and can no longer be avoided or considered unattainable. It is possible to carry the Presence of the

Holy Spirit so well that the Father is revealed to this orphaned planet. That satisfies the quest for divine purpose quite well. Doing exactly as He did is what Jesus had in mind when He commission us in John 20:21.

Learning to Focus

Psalm 37 is one of my favorite psalms. I turn to it frequently to feed on over and over again. In it, I discovered that waiting on the Lord was quite different from what I had originally thought. Waiting is not sitting still. It is more clearly seen in setting up an ambush for the one who promised, *"I will be found by you"* (Jer. 29:14). He wants to be found by us, but we must seek Him where He may be found. This is a place of rest that comes out of the conviction of who He is in us, and who we are in Him. For that reason, waiting makes sense. Verse 7 tells us to *"rest in the Lord and wait patiently for Him."* Resting is a beautiful picture of people that no longer feel the pressure to strive to prove themselves. They are comfortable in their own skin. (Before we're saved we performed to get an identity so we'd be accepted. After we're saved we find out we're accepted, and that's our identity, and from that reality comes our performance.)

Patiently has two meanings: "pain in childbirth" or "whirling in the air in dance." Both of these activities require incredible focus and strength. We are to wait on God with an unflinching resolve and focus, much like what Jacob had when he wrestled the angel. The same can be said of Elisha when he contended for Elijah's mantle.

There are seasons in life when being involved in many diverse activities is not only acceptable it's good. But there are also seasons when it is deadly. I was once driving from Northern California to Southern California on Interstate 5. South of Bakersfield I found myself in a dust storm that almost completely blinded me. It covered the entire freeway. There were cars immediately behind me, so I knew stopping could be disastrous. As I got into this cloud of dust I could faintly see cars and trucks scattered all over both sides of the freeway with people waving frantically. Talking with friends, listening to music, and the like are acceptable activities while driving, but they could have been deadly in this moment. Absolute silence filled the car as I worked to maintain my speed and focus on the lane ahead of me. After a minute or two, we made it through that terrifying cloud of death by God's grace alone.

Intense focus restricts what you are willing and able to see. And while this approach will keep you from seeing many things, it will also open your eyes to see more of what you hunger for. Self-control is not the ability to say no to a thousand other voices. It's the ability to say yes to the one thing so completely that there's nothing left to give to the other options.

The Holy Spirit is our greatest gift, and must become our single focus. With that in mind, each of us has become the target of God for a specific encounter that redefines our purpose on planet earth. It's the baptism of fire. We were born to burn. And while the danger of turning our attention from the person to the experience exists, it's worth the risk. No amount of miracles, no amount of insight, no amount of personal success will ever satisfy the cry of the heart for this baptism. And while many would like to just get it over with, often times there is a deep process involved. For the 120, it was ten days of continuous prayer. For me it was an eight-month season where my prayers actually woke me up. I didn't wake up to pray. I woke up praying.

Such a singleness of focus is rewarded. I personally don't think that these encounters are supposed to be a one-time event. We must have frequent encounters with God that continuously recalibrate our hearts that we might be entrusted with more and more of God.

What a person values they will protect. God will give us the measure of His presence that we are willing to jealously guard.

Historic Encounters

When Jesus appeared to two men on the road to Emmaus, He opened the Scriptures to explain why the Christ had to die. As yet they didn't know who He was, but they persuaded Him to stay for a meal. When He broke the bread, their eyes were opened, and then He vanished. Their response is one of my favorite ones in all of the Bible. *"Were not our hearts burning within us while He was speaking?"* (Luke 24:32). That is exactly what happens to me when I read of what this same Jesus has done in the lives of those who have given themselves for more. My hearts burns.

Below are a few stories of people and seasons in God. They are but a small handful of thousands that should be told.

Dwight L. Moody

It was some months later, while walking the streets of New York, that Dwight finally experienced the breakthrough for which he and Sarah Cooke had been praying together. It was shortly before his second and most important trip to England. R.A. Torrey had this to say about this significant advance in Moody's life:

Not long after, one day on his way to England, he was walking up Wall Street in New York; (Mr. Moody very seldom told this and I almost hesitate to tell it) and in the midst of the bustle and hurry of that city his prayer was answered; the power of God fell upon him as he walked up the street and he had to hurry off to the house of a friend and ask that he might have a room by himself, and in that room he stayed alone for hours; and the Holy Ghost came upon him, filling his soul with such joy that at last he had to ask God to withhold His hand, lest he die on the spot from very joy. He went out from that place with the power of the Holy Ghost upon him, and when he got to London, the power of God wrought through him mightily in North London, and hundreds were added to the churches; and that was what led to his being invited over to the wonderful campaign that followed in later years.

Dwight describes the experience in this way:

I was crying all the time that God would fill me with His spirit. Well, one day, in the city of New York—oh, what a day!—I cannot describe it, I seldom refer to it; it is almost too sacred an experience for to name. Paul had an experience of which he never spoke for fourteen years. I can only say that God revealed Himself to me, and I had such an experience of His love that I had to ask Him to stay His hand. I went to preaching again. The sermons were not different; I did not present any new truths, and yet hundreds were converted. I would not now be placed back where I was before that blessed experience if you should give me all the world—it would be as the small dust of the balance.[1]

Evan Roberts

For a period of time Evan had been seeking and finding a more intimate relationship with the Lord. William Davies, a deacon at the Moriah Chapel, had counseled young Evan never to miss the prayer meetings in case the Holy Spirit would come and

192

he would be missing. So Evan faithfully attended the Monday evening meeting at Moriah, Tuesday at Pisgah, Wednesday at Moriah, and Thursday and Friday at other prayer meetings and Bible classes. For thirteen years he did this and faithfully prayed for a mighty visitation for the Holy Spirit.

One day before school, in the spring of 1904, Evan found himself in what he later referred to as a Mount of Transfiguration experience. The Lord revealed himself in such an amazing and overwhelming manner that Evan was filled with divine awe. After this he would go through periods of uncontrollable trembling that brought concern to his family. For weeks God visited Evan each night. When his family pressed him to tell about the experiences he would only say it was something indescribable. When the time drew near for him to enter Grammar School at New Castle Emlyn, he was afraid to go because he was afraid that he would miss these encounters with the Lord.

At this time a convention was being held at Blaenenerch a few miles from his school. An evangelist named Seth Joshua was leading the meetings. On Thursday morning, September 29, 1904, Evan Roberts and 19 other young people, including his friend Sydney Evans, attended the meeting. On the way to the meeting the Lord moved on the small company and they began to sing: "It is coming, it is coming—the power of the Holy Ghost—I receive it—I receive it—the power of the Holy Ghost."

During the seven o'clock meeting Evan was deeply moved and he broke down completely at the close of the service. When Seth Joshua used the words *Bend us, oh Lord,* Evan entered such travail that he heard nothing more. He later testified that the Spirit of God whispered to him: "This is what you need."

"Bend me, Oh Lord," he cried. But the fire did not fall. At the 9 o'clock meeting the spirit of intercession was moving on the congregation in great power. Evan was bursting to pray. Then the Spirit of God told him to do so publicly. With tears streaming down his face Evan just began to cry: *"Bend me! Bend me! Bend me! Bend us'*. Then the Holy Spirit came upon him with a mighty baptism that filled Evan with Calvary's love and a love for Calvary. That night the message of the cross was so branded upon Evan's heart that there would be no other theme of the great revival he would soon help lead. From that night on Evan Roberts could focus on one thought—the salvation of souls. Historians would refer to that night as "Blaenanerch's great meeting."

One midnight shortly after this, Evan's roommate and closest friend, Sydney Evans, came into the room to find Evan's face shining with a holy light. Astonished, he asked what had happened. Evan replied that he had just seen in a vision the whole of Wales being lifted up to heaven. He then prophesied: "We are going to see the mightiest revival that Walker has ever known—and the Holy Spirit is coming just now. We must get ready. We must have a little band and go all over the country preaching." Suddenly he stopped and with piercing eyes he cried: *"Do you believe that God can give us 100,000 souls, now?"*

The presence of the Lord so gripped Sydney that he could not help but believe. Later, while sitting in a chapel, Evan saw in a vision some of his old companions and many other young people as a voice spoke to him saying: *"Go to these people."* He said, "Lord, if it is Thy will, I will go." Then the whole chapel became filled with light so dazzling that he could only faintly see the minister in the pulpit. He was deeply disturbed and wanted to make sure that this vision was of the Lord. He consulted with his tutor who encouraged him to go.[2]

Mel Tari

In the mid 1960s, Tari was sitting in his Presbyterian church as people were praying, when suddenly the Holy Spirit hit the place. Everyone began to audibly hear the sound of a mighty rushing wind filling the room. The village fire bell began ringing, and local firefighters rushed to the building. The church was covered in flames, but it was not burning. Many were saved that day. What began with a few dozen people would go on to impact the world.[3]

The Cevennes Prophets

(Seventeenth Century) The Cevennes prophets of France are an interesting case study in corporate Holy Spirit outpourings. God began an awakening in the Cevennes when in the 1688, 16 year-old Isabeau Vincent began to have ecstasies, shaking and fainting, wherein she could quote Scriptures she had never known and prophesy. She would sometimes sing or preach sermons in her sleep. She impacted many, leading them to repentance. Dozens of people in her village were ignited with a prophetic gifting, and as news spread, visitors flocked to the area. Many in the Cevennes had angelic visions, and they were sometimes led to secret meetings by means of lights in the sky. Specific words of knowledge were common, and all were driven to a thirst for holiness. People began to pray and fast, and their meetings were marked by unusual spontaneity, as well as exuberant and demonstrative worship. Physical manifestations of God's presence were also present on believers.[4]

The Moravians

The Moravians of Herrnhut, Saxony, were a group of about 300 refugees living on the estate of Count Nicholaus von Zinzendorf, when in 1727 a great outpouring of the Holy Spirit fell. "We saw the hand of God and His wonders, and we were all under the cloud of our fathers baptized with their Spirit. The Holy Ghost came upon us and in those days great signs and wonders took place in our midst. From that time scarcely a day passed but what we beheld His almighty workings amongst us."[5]

George Whitefield

Whitefield was a major player in the Great Awakening Started by Jonathan Edwards. Many were saved in his missions, and it is estimated that he preached to six million without the use of radio or television. Whitefield's meetings were criticized for their emotional expressions of worship. John Wesley describes a prayer meeting with Whitefield, in which the Spirit of God moved on them in 1739. "About three in the morning, as we were continuing instant in prayer, the power of God came mightily upon us, insomuch that many cried out for exceeding joy, and many fell to the ground. As soon as we were recovered a little from the awe and amazement at the presence of His majesty, we broke out with one voice, 'We praise Thee, O God, we acknowledge Thee to be the Lord.'" Understand that we are not referring to hype or a striving, emotional attempt to garnish experience from God. This is about the sudden, undeniable surprises of His sovereignty.[6]

William Seymour

The Spirit began to fall in Los Angeles, as people were radically filled and walked out into the streets speaking in tongues. Crowds began to grow at these home meetings, where Seymour was living with a host family. Before long, they were preaching from the front porch as people filled the streets to listen. Eventually, they moved into an old horse stable at 312 Azusa Street. It was in this stable in 1906 that the Pentecostal movement was officially born.

People would fall over and weep. They would speak in tongues. They would laugh, jerk, dance, and shout. They would wait on the Lord for hours, sometimes saying nothing. Seymour would often preach from his knees.

"No one could possibly record all the miracles that occurred there," writes charismatic historian Roberts Liardon. John G. Lake said of William Seymour that, "He had more of God in his life than any man I had ever met up to that time."

Prayer lasted all day and all night. Firemen were even dispatched to Azusa Street, because people saw a "fire," which was actually just the visible glory of God resting on the exterior of the building. Similar occurrences have happened in a number of revivals, like the Indonesian revival, as recorded by Mel Tari in the 1970s, where firemen were also dispatched to a "glory fire" that was visible to everyone around.

Missionaries began coming to Azusa Street from around the world to catch the fire. People would fall over, get saved and begin speaking in tongues blocks away from the building, even though no one prayed for them, and they had no idea what was going on in the Azusa mission. Parishioners would also hit the streets, knocking on doors with little bottles of oil and asking to pray for the sick.

Seymour sought first and foremost to cultivate the presence of God in his meetings. If someone felt led, they would stand up and begin to pray or preach. If the anointing did not seem to be on a particular speaker, that person would sometimes get a gentle tap on the shoulder to hush up. Truly, the Spirit of God was the leader of those meetings.[7]

John G. Lake

One afternoon a brother minister called and invited me to accompany him to visit a lady who was sick. Arriving at the home we found the lady in a wheelchair. All her joints were set with inflammatory rheumatism. She had been in the condition for ten years. While my friend was conversing with her, preparing her to be prayed with, that she might be healed, I sat in a deep chair on the opposite side of a large room. My soul was crying out to God in a yearning too deep for words, when suddenly it seemed to me that I had passed under a shower of warm tropical rain, which was not falling upon me but through me. My spirit and soul and body, under this influence, was soothed into such a deep still calm as I had never known. My brain, which had always been so active, became perfectly still. An awe of the presence of God settled over me. I knew it was God.

Some moments passed; I do not know how many. The Spirit said, "I have heard your prayers, I have seen your tears. You are now baptized in the Holy Spirit." Then currents of power began to rush through my being from the crown of my head to the soles of my feet. The shocks of power increased in rapidity and voltage. As these currents of power would pass through me, they seemed to come upon my head, rush through my body and through my feet into the floor. The power was so great that my body began to vibrate intensely so that I believe if I had not been sitting in such a deep low chair I might have fallen upon the floor.

At that moment I observed my friend was motioning me to come and join him in prayer for the woman who was sick. In his absorption he had not noticed that anything had taken place in me. I arose to go to him, but I found my body trembling so violently that I had difficulty in walking across the room, and especially in controlling the trembling of my hands and arms. I knew that it would not be wise to thus lay my hands upon the sick woman as I was likely to jar her. It occurred to me that all that was necessary was to touch the tips of my fingers on the top of the patient's head and then the vibrations would not jar her. This I did. At once the currents of holy power passed through my being, and I knew that it likewise passed through the one that was sick. She did not speak, but apparently was amazed at the effect in her body.

My friend who had been talking to her in his great earnestness had been kneeling as he talked to her. He arose saying, "Let us pray that the Lord will now heal you." As he did so he took her by the hand. At the instant their hands touched, a flash of dynamic power went through my person and through the sick woman, and as my friend held her hand the shock of power went through her hand into him. The rush of power into his person was so great that it caused him to fall on the floor. He looked up at me with joy and surprise, and springing to his feet said, "Praise the Lord, John, Jesus has baptized you in the Holy Ghost!"

Then he took the crippled hand that had been set for so many years. The clenched hands opened and the joints began to work, first the fingers, then the hand and the wrist, then the elbow and shoulder.

These were the outward manifestations. But Oh! Who could describe the thrills of joy inexpressible that were passing through my spirit? Who could comprehend the peace and presence of God that thrilled my soul? Even at this lade date, ten years afterward the awe of that hour rests upon my soul. My experience has truly been as Jesus said: *"He shall be within you a well of water, springing up into everlasting life."* That never-ceasing fountain has flowed through my spirit, soul and body day and night, bringing salvation and healing and the Baptism of the Spirit in the power of God to multitudes.[8]

Charles Finney

Charles Finney is one of the great revivalists in American history. While he is well-known for revival and his preaching of true repentance, not everyone recognizes him as a great social reformer. The emancipation of slaves and the rights of women were two of the issues that were heavily impacted through his preaching. The revivals were obviously to get people converted to Jesus Christ. But his target was far beyond filling churches with new members. He knew that if there was to be a lasting result to his preaching there had to be deep cultural change. All true preachers of the gospel must keep this in mind. But for the theme of this book, one story stands out head and shoulders above the rest. He writes of this unusual experience in his own autobiography.

He entered a factory one morning after breakfast. In a room filled with young ladies working on their weaving machines, looms, and spinning devices, two in particular stood out to him. They looked a bit agitated, but seemed to cover it with laughter. He said nothing, but walked closer, noticing that one was trembling so badly that she couldn't mend her thread. When he got to within about 8 to 10 feet they burst out in tears and slumped down. In moments nearly the whole roomful of workers was in tears. The owner, who was yet unconverted himself, recognized that this was a divine moment and ordered that his factory be shut down to give his workers a chance to come to Christ. A mini-revival broke out, which lasted several days. Nearly the entire mill was converted during this time. It all started with a man upon whom the Spirit of God loved to rest. And so without words a room full of workers came under the conviction of the Holy Spirit and a revival was born.

While this exact experience did not happen every day, I can't help but wonder if maybe the Lord is trying to draw us into a greater hunger for more, now that we know what else is possible. This testimony is in God's resume. It reveals how He is willing to affect the surroundings of those who host Him well.[9]

Smith Wigglesworth

Here is the final story that is my favorite story in this chapter. It is one of my favorite stories in all of church history. Smith was a man of the Presence.

> There were 11 leading Christians in prayer with our Brother at a special afternoon meeting. Each had taken a part. The Evangelist then began to pray for the Dominion, and as he continued, each, according to their measure of spirituality, got out. The power of God filled the room and they could not remain in an atmosphere supercharged by the power of God.
>
> The author on hearing of this from one who was present registered a vow that if the opportunity came, he at any rate would remain whoever else went out. During the stay in the Sounds a special meeting was called to pray for the other towns in New Zealand yet to be visited. A like position to the other meeting now arose. Here was the opportunity, the challenge, the contest was on. A number prayed. Then the old saint began to lift up his voice, and strange as it may seem, the exodus began. A Divine influence began to fill the place. The room became holy. The power of God began to feel like a heavy weight. With set chin, and a definite decision not to

budge, the only other one now left in the room hung on and hung on, until the pressure became too great, and he could stay no longer. With the flood gates of his soul pouring out a stream of tears, and with uncontrollable sobbing he had to get out or die; and a man who knew God as few do was left alone immersed in an atmosphere that few men could breathe in.[10]

Take Note

I hope you noticed that the stories of deep personal encounters resulted in outpourings, movements, societal transformation, and ultimately an increased awareness of His Presence, sometimes over a city, region, or nation. Those experiences affected everything about their lives and eventually impacted their surroundings. The historic transformations of culture didn't happen merely because people got into political office and made changes according to their convictions. While that can be good, there's something much better. Presence. These normal people became heroes of the faith, not because of their giftedness, their intelligence, or their pedigree. They are heroes because they learned the value of their greatest gift—the Holy Spirit.

What Now?

Stories like these make me feel like I've just entered that dust cloud on Interstate 5 again. But this time it's not the danger of an accident that has my eyes fixed on the road ahead. It's the chance I could miss the purpose for which I was apprehended by God by being preoccupied with other things. Lesser things. These stories are testimonies that prophesy of what God has made available for us in our lifetime. As such, they set a legal precedent. The courts of Heaven have concluded once and for all that the kind of life represented in the lives of these heroes of the faith is available for all.

We are the ones upon whom the promises of the ages have come to rest. And they are contingent upon our being a people who have discovered our eternal purpose. We have been chosen to be His eternal dwelling place. We have been chosen to host His Presence.

ENDNOTES

1   **Dwight L. Moody**
Roberts Liardon, *God's Generals: The Revivalists* (New Kensington, PA: Whitaker House, 2008), 366-367.

2   **Evan Roberts**
Rick Joyner, *The World Aflame: Guidance from the Greatest Revival Yet and the Greater One to Come*, (New Kensington, PA: Whitaker House, 1996), 35-37.

3   **Mel Tari (The New Mystics page 108)**
John Crowder, *The New Mystics*, (Shippensburg, PA: Destiny Image Publisher, 2006), 108.

4   **The Cevennes Prophets (The New Mystics Page 122)**
John Crowder, *The New Mystics*, (Shippensburg, PA: Destiny Image Publisher, 2006), 122.

5   **The Moravians (The New Mystics Page 169)**
John Crowder, *The New Mystics*, (Shippensburg, PA: Destiny Image Publisher, 2006), 169.

6   **George Whitefield**
John Crowder, *The New Mystics*, (Shippensburg, PA: Destiny Image Publisher, 2006), 171.

7   **William Seymour**
John Crowder, *The New Mystics*, (Shippensburg, PA: Destiny Image Publisher, 2006), 187-189 .

8 **John G Lake**
Gordon Lindsay, ed., *The Johns G. Lake Sermons on Dominion Over Demons, Disease, and Death* (Olendale, CA: The Bhurrh Press: Farson and Sons, 1949), 5-9, used by permission of Christ for the Nations, Inc., Dallas, TX.

9 **Charles Finney**
Charles G. Finney, *Memoirs of Rev. Charles G. Finney* (New York: A. S. Barnes & Company, 1896), 183-184.

10 **Smith Wigglesworth:**
H. V. Roberts, *New Zealand's Greatest Revival; Reprint of the 1922 Revival Classic: Smith Wigglesworth* (Dilsburg, PA: Rex Burger Books [www.klifemin.org], 1951), 46-47.

About Bill Johnson

Bill Johnson is a fifth-generation pastor with a rich heritage in the Holy Spirit. Together Bill and his wife serve a growing number of churches that have partnered for revival. This leadership network has crossed denominational lines, building relationships that enable church leaders to walk successfully in both purity and power.

Bill and Brenda (Beni) Johnson are the senior pastors of Bethel Church in Redding, California. All three of their children and spouses are involved in full-time ministry. They also have nine wonderful grandchildren.

IN THE RIGHT HANDS, THIS BOOK WILL CHANGE LIVES!

Most of the people who need this message will not be looking for this book. To change their lives, you need to put a copy of this book in their hands.

> But others (seeds) fell into good ground, and brought forth fruit, some a hundred-fold, some sixty-fold, some thirty-fold (Matthew 13:8).

Our ministry is constantly seeking methods to find the good ground, the people who need this anointed message to change their lives. Will you help us reach these people?

> Remember this—a farmer who plants only a few seeds will get a small crop. But the one who plants generously will get a generous crop (2 Corinthians 9:6).

EXTEND THIS MINISTRY BY SOWING
3 BOOKS, 5 BOOKS, 10 BOOKS, OR MORE TODAY,
AND BECOME A LIFE CHANGER!

Thank you,

Don Nori Sr., Founder
Destiny Image
Since 1982